Changing Curriculum through Stories

Changing Curriculum through Stories

Character Education for Ages 10–12

Marc Levitt

ROWMAN & LITTLEFIELD
Lanham • Boulder • New York • London

Published by Rowman & Littlefield
A wholly owned subsidiary of
The Rowman & Littlefield Publishing Group, Inc.
4501 Forbes Boulevard, Suite 200, Lanham, Maryland 20706
https://rowman.com

Unit A, Whitacre Mews, 26-34 Stannary Street, London SE11 4AB,
United Kingdom

British Library Cataloguing in Publication Information Available

Library of Congress Cataloging-in-Publication Data

ISBN: 978-1-4758-3590-8 (cloth : alk. paper)
ISBN: 978-1-4758-3591-5 (pbk. : alk. paper)
ISBN: 978-1-4758-3592-2 (electronic)

♾ ™ The paper used in this publication meets the minimum requirements of American
National Standard for Information Sciences Permanence of Paper for Printed Library
Materials, ANSI/NISO Z39.48-1992.

Printed in the United States of America

To Beverly, Richard, Kate, Talia, Joshua, and Ariana Levitt

Contents

Preface

In 1988 at the Democratic National Convention, then Texas agricultural commissioner Jim Hightower said that George H. W. Bush was a person "born on third base who thought he had hit a triple." While lampooning the president's privileged background and his ignorance about how his family's money and connections made his rise in politics possible, Hightower also inadvertently pointed out a blind spot in the American psyche, the mistaken belief that we live outside of our social and/or environmental context. This idea, that we are, as Paul Simon famously said, "rocks" and "islands," rather than rhizomes, birthed from and giving birth to, other roots and rhizomes, obfuscates how we are social creatures, needing each other for everything from intimacy to vocational success.

We are moved by the caring acts of others and empathize with their emotional struggles. We smile at a chance encounter with a "consequential stranger" and we are grateful for those whose lives touched ours in meaningful and inspiring ways. Yet, in spite of this, we hold tightly to our belief that we are autonomous creatures, living essentially without being affected by and not affecting others.

Consequently, in school, when we "teach" character education, it is too often through the use of admonition, as if we are trying to "tame the beast" in ourselves, rather than by building on our pro-social proclivities and our innate understanding that indeed, "we are all in it together."

In *Changing Curriculum through Stories: Character Education for Ages 10–12*, we will look at how our curriculum and its delivery supports the interpretation that we are inherently isolated and competitive individuals. Through stories, tips for classroom conversation, and curriculum and pedagogical suggestions, I will try to help educators help their students to recognize and act with the understanding that we are interdependent and that actions are not without consequences, both to others and to oneself.

At the age of twenty-three, after a childhood filled with idolizing heroic cowboys, soldiers, and baseball players and a teenage and early twenties filled with romance for great artists and revolutionary leaders, I believed I was destined to be yet another solitary hero. I wasn't very happy and felt isolated and trapped within my own thoughts, dreams, and aspirations.

One spring, 1973 day, in San Francisco, I left my work as a teacher in a "feminist/socialist parent co-op" and walked into a park and sat. I was locked inside a spinning fun house of thoughts, trapped in my own isolation. I was living inside a room of reflecting mirrors, captive of an unending loop of thoughts and questions. I asked myself the essential question, "Who am I?" and realized that my goals for my life were restricted by my romance for the autonomous heroes of my youth. I realized that if I continued to live in this way, I would live bereft of real human contact.

My goals were almost immediately transformed from those generated by what I call "Shallow Individualism," the belief that we are self-contained individuals operating in a world of other autonomous humans, to ones birthed by "Deep Individualism," the recognition that the true fulfillment of an individual life lies in the understanding that we are truly "all in it together." Personal fulfillment was no longer generated by a childhood dream of heroic isolation but upon recognizing and acting upon my permeability, vulnerability, and the need for others.

After a lifetime of working at the intersection of arts, humanities, and education, here is how I have come to look at how we, as educators, can help our students prepare for a world where interdependency is not only a philosophical concept, but an issue of individual well-being and indeed, planetary survival.

Introduction

It is difficult to judge how much of a problem bullying actually is. So much of it goes undetected in both manifestation and ramification, perpetrated behind corners, in secluded environments, through the Internet. So much gets unreported because of fear, its accepted "normality," and/or from the hope that it will eventually end.

Are bullying, teasing, and so forth more present now than ever, or are we just speaking about them more? Do new technologies and distribution systems like Facebook and Twitter make bullying more pervasive or are we exaggerating its extent? Are kids becoming less sensitive to others as their worlds become more confined to their homes and screens? Is the proliferation of adult-driven activities as opposed to "free" play in the neighborhood, rendering the skill of negotiating differences and compromise, vestigial, no longer needed when adults are making the rules? Is our nation's increasing income disparity and the anxiety it fosters leading to more stress within households, contributing to more violence outside?

These questions are probably unanswerable. Certainly, though, it is irrefutable that teasing and bystander behavior is occurring. Whether bullying is increasing or not and why is another book, one that requires a different competency than that of this author. Instead, this book is more interested in helping you to help your students understand that their well-being and the well-being of others are linked together and that acting from this understanding will benefit them at school, at home, and in their community. Additionally, this book is interested in helping educators be aware of how they are inadvertently helping to create the very behavior they want to eradicate, through what is being taught and how.

Student behavior as well as your school's curriculum is nested within a larger societal cultural narrative. Children internalize the behavior and behavioral expectations they see in adults and notice within the media. Young people make choices about who they are and how they are expected to behave through a complex dance that includes the instinctual, psychological, and social, all of whose borders are actually quite porous.

Curriculum is created, chosen, and distributed in ways that reflect everything from how its writers perceive the world, to the politics and economics of textbook adoption. Complex and at times contradictory narratives are built into what we "digest" through advertising; mass media; means of control at home, work, and play; as well as the content of a school's curriculum and the way it is distributed. These messages, subtle and not so subtle, affect everything from who we are and how we behave, to how we interpret what being "human" is all about.

In an August 2016 study by John Ifcher of Santa Clara University and Homa Zarghamee of Barnard College, "The Rapid Evolution of Homo Economics: Brief Exposure to Neoclassical Assumptions Increases Self-Interested Behavior," they found that "even brief exposure to commonplace neoclassical economics assumptions moves behavior toward self-interest."

In other words, the authors found that learning that self-interest—or better said, "shallow self-interest"—is "rational," led students to act "selfishly". It left little room for contemplating behavior embedded in an alternative understanding of our motives and proclivities, ones that foreground the common good and an awareness of our interdependency.

In spite of our well-intentioned interest in creating a positive school environment, one where harmony, peace, and diversity celebration are priorities, these goals are often contradicted and ultimately thwarted by the way these goals are shared and the content and distribution of the rest of the school curriculum. To be even partially successful in creating an atmosphere where student behavior is changed from "me first" to "your health is my health" we must align our pro-social messages with the content and distribution of the rest of the curriculum. As Marshall McLuhan said, "The medium is the message."

Our society's dominant cultural narrative, the story that frames how we think about who we are, what stories we tell about ourselves, and what motivates much of our behavior toward one another is a narrative that derives in large part from what I call "Shallow Individualism." This philosophy is based on our understanding that we are separate and discrete entities making our way in a world of other separate and discrete entities, in which "nature" is distinct from "self" and where we are in constant fear of shortage, calamity, and Hobbesian-type chaos.

This belief posits a competitive model to survive, one where there are winners and losers. Obviously this is not the complete story about how we perceive the world nor does it accurately depict how we behave. We care for our families, friends, neighbors, and coworkers and understand their importance in our lives. We are exalted by nature's beauty and understand how air and water pollution can affect our heath and happiness. Nonetheless, for the most part, in the United States, our national anthem, the song we march to, is essentially the "late period" Sinatra anthem, "My Way."

Individualism's emphasis on acting according to our own internal mandates is not without its important historical role. The freedom to set out on one's own, outside superstitious, unnecessarily restrictive, and often capricious boundaries, enforced by "inevitability," and/or physical and psychological power, based on class, caste, race, family, gender, sexual choice, and so on, was truly liberating.

In our contemporary society, however, Individualism has morphed into a perversion of a genuinely liberating philosophy. While Individualism had and probably still has an important role to play in freeing us from unnecessary and/or unwarranted restrictions, as well as serving as the basis for much of the Universal Principals of Human Rights, it has created a world in its most extreme image.

We have become blind to what we have in common, to how much we need one another, and to the effects our actions have on others and ultimately on ourselves. We have become blind to how all of our fates are linked. The power of "Shallow Individualism" has also obscured our innate understanding of how we learn socially, need each other for our happiness, and are in continuing dialogue with "nature."

"Shallow Individualism" is at the foundation of our curriculum and pedagogy. When we study history, we too often learn the stories of socially decontextualized "great" men (usually men and White men at that). We view nature as something outside of ourselves rather than with the understanding that we *are* nature, in continual dialogue with all else on this planet and probably beyond. We don't teach subjects from a systems or an ecological point of view, but instead teach as if one subject is separate from another. Our testing models are predicated on sorting and pitting one against the other, rather than on supporting cooperation and the success of all.

The results of teaching from this perspective is at variance with what we say we want to accomplish with our social curriculum; getting along, working together, and valuing differences. It's a contradiction to teach cooperation in a school where there are few opportunities to work cooperatively. It is very difficult to celebrate diversity when very few types of intelligences are venerated, utilized, or assessed; when the stories of so many are invisible. It is practically impossible to understand that actions have consequences when we teach subjects as impenetrable fortresses impervious to their "surroundings."

Our school culture, its pedagogy, and its curriculum not only reinforce our inherent competitiveness and our illusion of our own isolation, but also don't take advantage of our students' visceral understanding of empathy and their enjoyment of cooperation. Consequently, when teaching character education, we have no recourse but admonition and threats.

If we are to avoid an admonition-based, top-down approach in our attempts to create a sustainable culture of caring in our schools, we need to find ways to build upon our students' "better angels"; to reinforce our students' visceral understanding that the culture they create is the one they inhabit. This type of school finds ways to appreciate and utilize the talents of all, to render visible cause and effect and the permeability of illusory "borders" and teaches intellectually and viscerally, how we are, as a species, equally, if not more so, predisposed to cooperation than we are to competition.

The good news is that in science and human relationship theory, it is becoming more and more acknowledged that our happiness and well-being *is* dependent upon each other's happiness and well-being and that it is as "natural" to cooperate as it is to compete, both in human and animal worlds. We are connected biologically and psychologically and just as we are hardwired for competition, we are also hardwired for cooperation, compassion, forgiveness, altruism, generosity, and empathy and in fact our survival has long depended upon it. Here is some literature that supports this point of view:

- In two anthologies, *Prosocial Motives, Emotions and Behavior: The Better Angels of our Nature*, edited by Mario Mikulincer and Phillip R. Shaver (American Psychological Association, 2010) and *The Compassionate Instinct: The Science of Human Goodness* , edited by Dacher Keltner, Jeremy Adam Smith, and Jason Marsh (W. W. Norton & Company, 2010), the authors write about research into these and other areas of what is often referred to as "Pro-Social Behavior," behavior that derives from our innate and perhaps even genetically encoded understanding of how important it is for our species' survival to simply get along and cooperate.
- In Rebecca Solnit's superb book, *A Paradise Built in Hell: The Extraordinary Communities That Arise in Disaster* (Viking Adult, 2009) she looks at how after our twentieth-century natural and human-made disasters, individuals spontaneously formed "communities of help" without government aid. Ironically, soon after they did, "forces of order" like the military, whose homes were far from affected communities, with little or no contact with local residences and who operated from a Hobbesian paradigm, interpreted these communities of help as possible sites for anarchy. Expecting the worst of people in crisis, they shut down many of these helping communities and imposed a "top-down" model of aid.
- Matt Ridley's *The Origins of Virtue* (Penguin Books; Paperback 1st edition 1998) argues that cooperation and self-interest are not in conflict.
- In *A Cooperative Species* (Princeton University Press; Reprint edition, 2013), Samuel Bowles and Herbert Gintis discuss how society builds institutions around altruism and cooperation to perpetuate itself.

- Christopher Boehm, director of the Jane Goodall Research Center and professor of anthropology, in *Moral Origins: The Evolution of Virtue, Altruism, and Shame* (Basic Books, 2012) looks at how our morality has evolved as a necessity and often through peer disapproval with antisocial behavior as a survival technique.
- Paul Seabright in *The Company of Strangers: A Natural History of Economic Life* (Princeton University Press, 2010) looks at how trust and interconnectivity are evident in the species even within finance and our vast networks that produce and distribute our needs.
- Elinor Ostrom, the first woman to receive a Nobel Prize in economics, in *Governing the Commons: The Evolution of Institutions for Collective Action* (Cambridge: Cambridge University Press, 1990) studied how individuals in different parts of the world work together to prevent the destruction of what they have in common.
- Frans de Waal is a primatologist and ethologist. *Peacemaking Among Primates* (Harvard University Press; Reprint edition 1990) perhaps locates the biological roots to conflict and reconciliation and looks at the peacekeeping techniques of primates.
- Yochai Benkler's book *The Wealth of Networks* (Yale University Press, 2007) looks at how informational technology supports and itself is based upon collaboration. He cites *Wikipedia*, Creative Commons, Open Source Software, and the blogosphere as examples.
- David Bollier, an American activist, writer, and policy strategist, has written a number of books on the commons, that is to say, what we share, utilize, and collectively take care of for our mutual advantage.

When Nicholas A. Christakis, a physician and sociologist and professor at Harvard University, and James Fowler, an internationally recognized political scientist who is an associate professor of political science at the University of California, San Diego, announced their finding of a study they made about the roots of happiness with a group of 4,739 people followed from 1983 to 2003, as part of the famous Framingham Heart Study, it sent waves through the mainstream media.

> Our happiness is determined by a complex set of voluntary and involuntary factors, ranging from our genes to our health to our wealth. Alas, one determinant of our own happiness that has not received the attention it deserves is the happiness of others. Yet we know that emotions can spread over short periods of time from person to person, in a process known as "emotional contagion." If someone smiles at you, it is instinctive to smile back. If your partner or roommate is depressed, it is common for you to become depressed.
>
> But might emotions spread more widely than this in social networks— from person to person to person, and beyond? Might an individual's location within a social network influence their future happiness? And might social

network processes—by a diverse set of mechanisms—influence happiness not just fleetingly, but also over longer periods of time?

[The people they studied were] embedded in a larger network of 12,067 people; they had an average of 11 connections to others in the social network (including to friends, family, co-workers, and neighbors); and their happiness was assessed every few years using a standard measure.

We found that social networks have clusters of happy and unhappy people within them that reach out to three degrees of separation. A person's happiness is related to the happiness of their friends, their friends' friends, and their friends' friends' friends—that is, to people well beyond their social horizon. We found that happy people tend to be located in the center of their social networks and to be located in large clusters of other happy people. And we found that each additional happy friend increases a person's probability of being happy by about 9%. For comparison, having an extra $5,000 in income (in 1984 dollars) increased the probability of being happy by about 2%.

Happiness, in short, is not merely a function of personal experience, but also is a property of groups. Emotions are a collective phenomenon. (www. edge.org/3rd_culture/christakis_fowler08/christakis_fowler08_index.html)

These books and this study are rooted in an understanding that we are connected to one another and that our well-being depends upon the well-being of others. If we as educators base our teaching styles, our pedagogy, and our content on this understanding, we can change our school environment and dare I say it, our global culture, to one where happiness, success, safety, and the fulfillment of being human can be derived not from competition, not from a fear-based model, but from one that supports our inherent connection to all that we are linked to.

We will probably never be able to completely eliminate bullying, teasing, snubbing, passive bystander behavior, and so on, but we can help our students understand that it is not the only strategy available to survive and indeed to flourish.

A short story: Five poor brothers who lived and always ate dinner together could only afford four rolls each day from the market. Each dinner was a source of anxiety. Each brother plotted ways to get one of the four rolls and not be the one who was left with none. It was not unlike a game of musical chairs. Dinner was *never* pleasant! One day a stranger passed through the village, knocked on their door, and asked if he might spend the night and have some dinner. The brothers looked at each other and their immediate thought was, "Now, instead of one being left without a roll, two would be!"

They got progressively more and more nervous just thinking about this. As they sat at the table, the brothers were twitching with anxiety as if they were at the starting line of a race. Each brother was anxiously waiting to grab a roll. Suddenly, the stranger reached out both hands and took the rolls, putting all four of them on his plate. The brothers sat silently, aghast at this stranger's audacity. Suddenly the stranger took his knife and cut each of the four rolls into half and then two of those halves, he cut in half. He gave a half a roll to each brother and to himself. Then to each, he gave the smaller portion, so each of those around the table got three quarters of a roll.

The brothers looked at each other and smiled at how lucky they were to get not only one piece of a roll but two! From that time on, each of the brothers got something and none were left without! Everyone agreed that after that, dinners were a lot more fun!

Please, let's not get caught up in whether or not this "enlightened" solution to the above problem could ever really be achieved in "real life." The point of this story is to demonstrate the differences in approaches between Shallow and Deep Individualism, between a solution based on short-term gain and one based on an understanding of "Mutuality of Interest." Whether or not it is possible to ever get your class, grade, school, community, nation, and/or world to behave according to the latter is impossible to predict. To make space for its possibility is what is important.

This book is about helping you think about, plan, and distribute a curriculum that makes visible how one person's well-being is ultimately another's. *Changing Curriculum through Stories: Character Education for Ages 10–12* suggests curriculum and pedagogical changes that will help your students recognize that bullying, teasing, isolating, passive bystander behavior, and expressing and acting upon fears about all kinds of diversity is not just "bad" but ultimately not in anyone's best interest. This book is about helping you create a curriculum and a method for its dissemination that will help your students remember that we are all social beings who need each other to learn, play, survive, and create to reach our fullest potential.

Changing Curriculum through Stories: Character Education for Ages 10–12 is not a book filled with admonition, but rather, a book that attempts to make an understanding of "Mutuality of Interest," the guiding principal in the behavior of students. It is a book of theory and of practice; giving a philosophical foundation to its point of view, while making very practical suggestions. Its goal is to help students make behavioral choices where individual goals and the needs of others no longer seem contradictory.

Culture change is not simple and can't be accomplished only through posters, speeches, and/or an occasional speaker. It needs to be embedded into the everyday interactions between student and student, teacher and student, staff and student, between your administration and faculty, into your curriculum, and woven into your pedagogical approach.

HOW CAN YOU USE THIS BOOK?

In *Changing Curriculum through Stories: Character Education for Ages 10–12*, there are personal narratives as well as original, folkloric-type stories about a variety of topics pertinent to character and social issues. There are stories about bullying, teasing, gossiping, rumors, snubbing, bystander behavior, boy-girl relationships, forgiveness, vengeance, diversity, empathy, cooperation, stubbornness, embarrassment, and sharing. After each story there are questions for students to think, write, and talk about pertaining to the issues addressed. There are also suggestions about how to integrate the lessons of these stories into your curriculum and its delivery system. You can pick stories at random, or read the stories in the order that I have given them.

May you enjoy using this book and that after you do, may admonitions like, "Do unto others as you would have them do unto you" and "Ye reap what ye sow" become no longer Sunday school platitudes, but as real as a cement truck. Karma is physical and tangible, whether or not you believe that the results of one's action will come in this life or another.

Good luck.

Chapter One

Andrea's Party and How Gary Became Part of a Conspiracy Not to Attend One

Walking into his classroom on the first day of sixth grade, Gary noticed that, once again, it all felt new and clean. It happened like this every year. At the end of the school year, in late June, things in PS 265 looked a little worn, with posters ripped at their bottoms; desks never quite making it into the perfectly straight, marching-soldier–like lines they were supposed to be in; floors scraped and stained; closets with a film of dust; and a teacher who looked like the room—basically OK but slightly worn.

At the beginning of the school year, though, the room shined with hope. The sun streamed in like stage lights in a theater, calling the eye's attention to the cleanliness of each and every part of the room. The floors were polished, desks were cleaned of pen and pencil marks, and thumbtacks and Scotch tape that held fraying posters on the walls in June were removed. No trace of the class that had occupied this room the previous year was visible.

Their teacher for sixth grade was Mrs. Howard, known by all for her friendship with last year's teacher, Miss McDougald. They would eat lunch together every day—two elderly teachers sitting, eating yogurt in the front of the room as the class came back from lunch.

Gary looked around, and everyone from last year's class was back. For some reason, their class had been kept together every year from third grade until now. As they entered the last year of their elementary school careers, they all realized (happily in some cases, sadly in others, and with a mix of feelings in still others) that this would be their final year together before merging into the big and unpredictable world of junior high.

A quick look around the room, and Gary noticed that the two months or so of summer vacation had changed everyone, some a little and some a lot. Some of the girls had grown taller, like Cheryl and Joan, who left the boys behind with their spurts of growth. Andrew had a dark growth of hair at the bottom of his nose, a growth that not too many years later would become a high-schooler's mustache, and Joyce—ah, Joyce!—she seemed even cooler and more in demand than last year, if that could be possible.

All the girls and some of the guys gathered around her. She was like a celebrity amid fawning paparazzi. She was giggling, telling everyone how good they looked, and talking about the summer she had spent at a camp in the Catskills, where she had an older boyfriend, a counselor in training.

Joyce, as you can guess, was the class's queen bee. Every class has one: the coolest, most knowing girl in the school. She had an older brother and sister and, because of that, learned from them. She just had a way of walking, acting, and knowing about the right clothes to wear, the right music to listen to, *and* even how to dance!

Gary's friend Everett matched Joyce for coolness. He had arrived in our school in fourth grade like a cowboy coming into a small, dusty Western town desperate for change. He had come from an exotic state (Kentucky), where they had horses and the Kentucky Derby. Everett was taller than everyone; talked in a strange drawl of an accent; and was perfectly polite and, like I said, unfailingly cool. They were royalty.

Everett danced with Joyce at all the parties, and Everett walked Joyce home after school. Gary confided to a few of the guys that Everett wasn't too happy Joyce had a boyfriend during the summer, but he had forgiven her. He realized that he couldn't hold a grudge because he had a girlfriend back in Kentucky, where he spent the summer with his father. So, they were now back together, and as Gary looked around at the newly clean, shiny room, the world seemed to be in its correct order.

The beginning of school went along with usual predictability. Mrs. Howard was an improvement from the imperial Miss McDougald but not by much. Mrs. Howard stood tall and regal. She demanded perfection, especially in penmanship. Her cursive writing on the blackboard looked better than the manufactured penmanship charts above.

Mrs. Howard's demand for perfection, as well as her assignments, felt like part of a secret plan to prepare her students for the rigors of junior high school and were a studied attempt to help them leap from childhood into the first scent of being grown-ups. During the year, there would be the homework assignments aligned with this effort; reports to do on the nations of the world; the French lessons by the French teacher, who would desperately try to get her students, children of the American dream, to believe that a language other than English was important; and, of course, lessons in fractions and equations.

Then, most importantly, there was real life, the life of the kids, the life that belonged only to them that they couldn't wait to get back to after the million interruptions forced on them by either teachers or parents. There were the punch-ball games, the basketball games, the football games, and the bowling league. There were the visits to girl's houses after school, girls who combed their hair and giggled with each other as music played from old 45s. There were the Western and World War II movies they'd go to on Saturdays and the parties in the basements of those lucky enough to have private houses in this land of apartment buildings.

There was the predictable and then, as always, the surprises, like that day in mid-November when Mr. Tauchner, the principal, came into their room with a girl neither Gary, nor anyone else had never seen before. All teaching stopped, and Mrs. Howard, who seemed prepared for this interruption, stopped diagramming sentences and asked that they give Mr. Tauchner their *full* attention.

"Hello, boys and girls," said Mr. Tauchner. "I see you are all working very hard, and I am sorry to bother you, but I'd like to introduce you to a girl who will be part of our school and of your class. Please welcome Andrea Kubek." Andrea smiled reluctantly, looking like she wished she was any-where else but there.

"Hi, Andrea," they said in bored uniformity. With that, Andrea was part of their worlds, both the public world of school and the secret world of kids.

Now, you might think that a new girl coming into a classroom filled with kids who had been together for three and a half years would have a difficult time adjusting. Maybe Andrea did, but she didn't seem to. Her behavior was easy, natural, like a good ice skater in a skating rink, not conceited but with a sense of knowing who she was and being comfortable with it. She was polite and interested in everyone, and they couldn't help but reciprocate. The girls invited her to movies, to do homework, and to go shopping, and she was brought seamlessly into all their games and laughter.

The trouble began—and you had to know there was going to be some—soon after Everett told Gary that he thought Andrea was pretty. Gary had not really thought of her in that way. While he certainly noticed girls back then, Gary's interests were the New York Yankees, playing sports, his guy friends, and then girls, in that order. There was, he had to admit, a freshness to her, like that classroom in September.

Things began to change between Everett and Andrea soon after his ad-mission. Andrea and Everett were talking together more at lunch and recess. Everett missed his friends' punch-ball games just to hang around Andrea. Soon, Everett stopped walking home with Joyce or with anyone else from the class. When Gary asked him why, he just shrugged his shoulders, but it wasn't long before the whole class realized that Everett had started to walk Andrea home after school.

The next day, Jeff, a red-haired boy with a face full of freckles, came up to Gary and whispered in a way that seemed like he was sharing some secret code for a bomb: "I just heard that Joyce found out that her cousin went to

Andrea's last school, and the reason she left was that she was thrown out because she had stolen money from someone's desk."

A day or so later, Gary heard a couple of girls talking: "Yeah, I always thought something was wrong. Why did she leave one school and come to another in the middle of school year? It just didn't make sense."

A few days later, Chris, a boy whose blond hair pointed up in the air like porcupine quills, came up and said to Gary, "What do you think of Andrea getting the whole class in trouble in her old school by telling the teacher they had all cheated on the test? Joyce told me." Ruth overheard what he had said and added, "Plus, Joyce heard from her cousin that Andrea steals everyone's boyfriend just for fun and then dumps them!"

It was strange what happened next. Predictable, Gary figured, but still strange. Here's what happened: Pretty soon the girls and some of the boys who had gathered around Andrea suddenly and for no apparent reason disappeared. Talk about the silent treatment! Andrea couldn't even get an "Excuse me" as kids brushed against her to take the last seat at the lunch table or as they rushed out of school on Friday afternoons. In gym, she was never chosen for a team, and in the hallway, walking to lunch, she did so alone. Pretty much it was only Everett who kept her company.

Soon her mother began to pick her up at school. Gary noticed that Andrea was hugged by her mother each time they met in the school office, and each day when she left, Andrea would have tears in her eyes.

One Monday, about two weeks later, for some reason things seemed suddenly better for Andrea. She came into school smiling and happy and a lot more confident, and in her hand were invitations she gave to everyone in class. They were invitations for a party Andrea was having at her house the following Friday night. They were handwritten. The invitation said, "Party next Friday night. My house. Food, games, and dancing!"

There is something about getting an invitation that makes people happy. They feel special being invited somewhere, and the fact that there would be dancing made it even better. Even though a lot of the kids in class pretended that those of the opposite sex were not really that important, now, by the middle of sixth grade, they all realized that they actually were. They even played the occasional spin the bottle and postman, where kisses were delivered as they disappeared briefly into a closet with someone who had been picked by random.

By Thursday, the whole class was feeling the excited buzz of the upcoming party, and now, once again, Andrea was included—included in the laughter, lunch tables, and walks in the hall down to gym and out of the school at the end of the day. Joyce watched with boiling anger as Andrea got back into the good graces of those who were supposed to be *her* domain. As the day of the party approached, Joyce's face got redder and redder. Her idea to isolate

Andrea failed as the party became the most important part of everyone's minds and conversation.

Joyce wasn't done, however. It was recess after lunch, and usually the boys played punch ball and the girls hung around and talked. Gary noticed that no one went to the field to play, but rather, both boys and girls congregated around Andrea. Everett stayed away, and Gary went to see what was going on. One by one, with Joyce watching like a theater director, they went over to Andrea and each made up an excuse why they couldn't go to the party.

"I'd like to go to your party, Andrea, but I feel that I'm getting sick."

"My cousin is coming in that day from France."

"My father's car is broken."

"I don't have shoes."

After everyone left, Andrea put her head down and walked away silently.

Chris walked by Gary after giving his excuse. "Why is everyone giving an excuse why they can't go to the party?" Gary asked.

He looked a bit embarrassed. "Joyce said that, if we went to the party, we wouldn't be invited to any parties next year."

The day of the party had arrived. As far as Gary knew, it was only he and Everett still going. Gary was getting ready to go, putting on his shirt, when he heard the doorbell ring. His father announced, "It's Everett."

"Hey, Gary. Let's go."

Suddenly, the phone rang. It was Joyce.

"Hi, Gary. Hey, you will never guess who I saw today on Austin Street. Vicki Terry. You know, that really pretty new girl in Mrs. Gibson's class? Guess what? She told me that she liked you. So, I decided that I would have a party at my house, invite just a few special friends, like you, and then invite her so that you both can—Oh, wait a minute. I can't invite you. Have a good time at Andrea's, Gary."

Gary slowly hung up the phone, and his head was spinning like a top.

"Hey, Gary, let's go!" called out Everett.

The next couple of seconds felt like an hour to Gary, who was suspended in indecision, feeling like a tightrope-walker crossing between two large buildings.

"Come on, Gary! Come on!"

Gary paused for a second, and then, suddenly and surprisingly, these words came out of his mouth: "My stomach hurts, Ev. You better just go to the party without me."

Gary was stunned by his own words. He hardly knew who said them. All he knew was that, a moment later and without saying anything else, he heard the door slam, and Everett left. Gary just stood there with his shirt half on and half off, unable to move.

The next day Everett returned. He seemed to be in a good mood.

"How was the party?" Gary asked.

"Good. No one showed up, and I got to eat all the candy!"

Life went on. The atmosphere in the class on Monday and for a couple of weeks afterward was a bit like a deflated balloon. No one talked about why. Maybe everyone was just carrying around feelings about the party, why they didn't go to, and how they felt about it.

The months passed by. Assignments were done. The school year ended. Summer laid out its carpet of fun, and in September, they all went to junior high. Some from elementary school stayed friends, and others didn't. Some were in the same classes, others nodded to each other in the halls, and some didn't bother to acknowledge one another.

It turned out that Gary became kind of friendly with Andrea. They eventually shared a couple high school classes, and both wrote for the school newspaper. She became, as Gary did, an editor of the paper. Both were on the school council.

Eventually, colleges were applied to. Acceptances and rejections were sent out. Then came college, and for a few years afterward, Gary would see and talk with Andrea at parties or reunions. For a long time, he didn't see her at all. But, one day, walking through New York City on his way to a movie, there she was: Andrea.

Andrea was with a man and a couple kids. Gary guessed they were her husband and children. Both were happy to see one another, and after the introductions to her family, they spoke for maybe five minutes, a sort of fast-forward summary of their lives. She had a good job as writer for a local arts newspaper and had written a book on a rock star who had gone to their high school.

Gary filled her in on his life. They promised to see each other more often and talked about organizing a reunion of their friends from high school. Gary gave Andrea a hug and said goodbye to her and her husband and kids. They walked away like two balloons dancing in the wind that had come together for a brief instant before going on their separate ways.

Gary was halfway down the block, thinking of Andrea and their meeting, when suddenly he began to run back toward her. She was walking with her family, oblivious to what was about to happen.

"Andrea!" Gary called out.

She turned around.

"Gary, you're back," she said, smiling.

Gary looked at her, paused for a second, and said, "Andrea, I have always wanted to apologize for not going to that party that you gave. I'm sorry."

She gave him a funny look. "What party, Gary?"

"The one you gave the year you first came into our class in elementary school."

"Oh, that one. I forgot all about it. It was really bad, that's for sure, but it is long gone from my head. But, thanks."

They hugged each other once again and walked away. He realized at that moment that, even though she had forgotten all about that party, he never would be able to forget it.

QUESTIONS FOR STUDENTS

- Would you have gone to Andrea's party if you were in Gary's shoes? Why or why not?
- Did you think Gary was going to go to the party? Why? Were you surprised by his decision? If so, why?
- Have you ever passed rumors about someone? Tell us what you said, when, about whom, and what affect it had on that on the person and on those you shared the rumor with.
- Have you ever had rumors passed about you? If so, how did you feel?
- Have you ever done something to someone you were not proud of? What was it? Did you think about it a lot afterward? Did you apologize to him or her? Would you like to?
- Do you remember a time when suddenly it seemed that no one liked you? Tell us about it.
- What, if anything, can you do if you hear someone passing rumors?
- Have you ever been so jealous of someone that you would have done anything to make him or her lose what they had and you had wanted? If so, did you do something to them that you now regret and if so, what?
- How could one person have so much power over others as they did at the school in this story?
- Can you really "steal" someone's boyfriend or girlfriend?

THOUGHTS FOR STUDENTS

This story is about how we can be affected negatively by choices we imagine are in our self-interests. We might know they are poor choices to make, but we do them anyway, thinking that we will be immune from their effects. This is also a story about rumors and jealousy.

How should Gary have acted when faced with Joyce's behavior and threats? Should he have said something to support Andrea against the rumors shared by Joyce and spread by his classmates? Should he have risked not being able to go to Joyce's party by going to Andrea's? Looking back, it certainly seems so. Had just a couple people refused to go along with the party boycott or with the passing of rumors, Joyce's power to dictate the class's behavior might have greatly decreased. Joyce's power was based on her confidence that everyone would be scared of the repercussions if they didn't do as she wanted.

If only a few kids would have refused to go along with Joyce's plan, everyone would have felt stronger to resist. Sometimes it takes just a couple people or even only one to stand up to someone whose power depends on creating a feeling that everyone is in agreement. To act courageously and morally can be very difficult. Certainly, Joyce's power over everyone's social life was difficult to ignore, but believe me, if just one person had resisted "going along to get along," it would have made it easier for all of them to act differently.

Swimming against the current is not easy. Going against power is not without a cost. We risk isolation, teasing, and worse, and yet, from experience, I've found that standing up for what you know is right makes you feel good about yourself. That feeling stays with you much longer than the momentary satisfaction of acting against your better instincts. It's the difference of eating a bag of potato chips at 6:00 p.m. versus having a good meal. One is temporarily satisfying, and the other is nourishing for the long term.

How can you find the strength to make choices that will benefit you in the long run while knowing that you risk the disapproval of your friends? For one thing, we need to notice and remember how we feel when we see others being picked on, snubbed, and gossiped about. There are very few young or old people who don't feel another person's suffering. Trust that feeling. Ask yourself how you can help. Can you refuse to pass a rumor? Can you ask others to stop teasing? Can you invite the person being snubbed to be part of a conversation or a game?

Sure! All of these choices would help the person being picked on or about whom the rumors are told and ultimately will make you feel better, too. Remember, when you go along with the crowd at the expense of another, you feel small, and when you refuse to go along and instead carve out an independent way to behave, one that helps another, you feel bigger.

While we all have to come to decisions about how to behave on our own, it helps to have a community of kids behind you who share the same values and priorities. How can you create that? How can you and your friends make some kind of pact not to support negative behavior toward others? How can you and your friends set up an environment in your school, your schoolyard, and beyond that brings people together, that makes everyone feel good, and that creates great feelings and memories for everyone? Can you read books together about these subjects? Can you learn from history about times when people stuck up for each other? Can you set up some storytelling sessions where kids tell their own stories about what it felt like to be bullied, to bully, to tease, to have been snubbed, to have passed a rumor, or to have been the victim of them?

Simply communicating about these issues will help. By doing so, you will create a group of friends who have the courage to do the right thing and to help each other do the same. Courage comes from inside, but it can be encouraged by others who understand that they are not only helping others but helping themselves, as well. A community of caring understands that what is best for someone else is ultimately best for everyone.

THOUGHTS FOR TEACHERS

Curriculum and Pedagogical Suggestions: Social Studies, English, Critical Thinking, and Media Studies

A story like this probably brings back unfortunate memories, doesn't it? How can you help students behave in a way that supports classroom harmony through an understanding of the long-term implications of this kind of behavior?

American history is unfortunately not without lessons in this regard. As you know, there was a period in American history when, if you were even suspected of having connections to the Communist Party, it could lead to being fired and socially and vocationally isolated. Often these accusations didn't even have to be substantiated, just rumored.

Many in this McCarthy period (named for Senator Joseph McCarthy, who spearheaded this effort) were brought in front of the House Un-American Activities Committee (HUAC) and were asked to testify against the people they worked with, went to parties with, or knew through friends or even acquaintances. Some of these many famous people who were brought before this committee gave the committee names of suspected Communists or Communist sympathizers, while others refused to testify. Some testified to save their own skins and some because they felt committed to the cause of getting rid of anyone who was tinged with Communism, past or present.

This became one of the United States' great moral issues in the early to mid-1950s. At that time, Arthur Miller wrote a now-famous play called *The Crucible*. It drew a connection between the McCarthy hearings and the Salem witch trials, another period when rumors and innuendos could lead to isolation and, in the case of the Witch Trials, hanging.

What happens when there is a collective unwillingness to challenge rumors? On the macrolevel, we can look at the McCarthy hearings, the witch trials of Salem, or the fear of being reported for Western sympathies in the 1950s through the 1980s while living in the Soviet Bloc. Within the Soviet orbit, even an anonymous report of the sound of an outlawed radio show could trigger an official investigation!

This mass culture of paranoia is aided and abetted by a society that is afraid to challenge the veracity or morality of passing rumors. This kind of social control mechanism gets its power from complicity, from those who believe that if they raise their voices against these rumors and their repercussions, then they, too, could become suspects and possibly suffer its consequences.

In this story, Joyce got her power in the same way: through fear. Because of this fear, the students in this story also lost all critical thinking facilities. No one asked if the rumors were true. No one challenged the source. Joyce's motives went unquestioned. This collective willingness to continue the string of unchallenged rumors helped create a horrible situation for a new member of that class and fostered a culture of fear in the classroom and long-term guilt for Gary and probably others.

By studying periods in history when rumor-mongering unfairly changed many people's lives and when a culture of paranoia was allowed to prevail within a community, it will help make similar, more personal situations visible to your students. This will help them think critically about not only the veracity of rumors but also about whether they should be passed or, indeed, challenged.

Think of the debates you could have when students are asked to discuss whether those accused of Communist sympathies should have been removed from jobs! Another interesting and entertaining angle to stimulate discussion is simply by playing the game of telephone, helping students realize that information that starts in one place often morphs beyond recognition by the time it reaches another's ears. Consider these efforts vaccines against rumor-passing.

Your students also need to be aware that there is no neutral stance when it comes to being a rumor-passer, a snubber, or one who let's rumors go unchallenged. Compliance and noncompliance is a choice, one with consequences for all and one with a great legalistic history in our country. The presumption of innocence is one of the most important pillars of our legal system. Teaching your students about why and how our legal system is based on this principle will help them realize that, by protecting the innocence of others, they are protecting themselves.

Creating a culture of critical thinking in your classroom is again a vaccination against the pervasive power of rumors. As any teacher or librarian knows, one of the first things taught about research is to question the source. In the library, students learn to check if a site is commercial in order to see if the creator of that site might have some ulterior motive for the information they share.

In the same way a site can have an ulterior motive, a person initiating a rumor can have one. Helping students learn how to discern the veracity of a source provides a needed distance from the herd mentality that blinds us as we go along to get along.

Questioning the source and noticing the gaps in a narrative are sources of strength for a student's ethical immune system. It creates a culture of intelligent skepticism in the classroom. Knowing how to find gaps in the narrative is also important for developing writers. Good writers are those who have given their readers all the information needed for their story or article to make sense. The skill of knowing which ingredients in a story are missing for their writing's coherency can be taught in fun, interesting, and challenging ways.

Study and role-play the work of lawyers, journalists, and detectives. Read detective stories, watch films, and read books about trials. Stop midway through any of these to predict endings and give reasons for these predictions. Initiate a classroom discussion in which students try to find the faults in their classmates' logic. These exercises help students fine-tune their questioning skills and learn not to jump to conclusions. They teach students to continually test the veracity of what they hear and to be skeptical of even their own initial conclusions.

A critical mind is an open mind. An open mind is a curious mind. A curious mind is a self-reflective mind. A self-reflective mind doesn't jump to conclusions, but rather looks at the consequences of doing so.

Chapter Two

Long John Skinny

Too Tall and Thin or Was He?

John was his real name, but he was called Long John Skinny for reasons easy to guess. He had arms that looked like garden hoses, legs of a daddy long-legs, and a neck that appeared to grow even as you looked at it. Long John Skinny lived in a neighborhood where talking about and playing sports was what life was about. Long John always wanted to be included and very rarely was.

It's not like Long John didn't hang out with the other kids, though. He'd sit with everyone as they'd eat Italian ices. He'd flip baseball cards and talk sports. Again, it's not like Long John wasn't kind of part of the group. It is just that he wasn't really fully accepted, and at the same time, more often than not, he was the one others made jokes about, the one who was inside because he seemed not to mind that he was really outside, always giving others someone to laugh at without complaint.

Long John would ask, "Can I play basketball today with you guys?" and one of the guys, Mike, kind of the local leader, would answer, "You can't play with us Long John because your arms look like toothpicks!"

Or Long John would say, "Can I play football with you guys today?"

Mike would say, "You can't play with us, Long John. You've got legs that look like telephone wires."

"Can I play baseball?"

"You can't play with us, Long John. You've got a neck that looks like a straw."

Everyone would laugh, play, and afterward talk about the game. Long John would always try to add some comment about the game he had watched but wasn't part of.

One of the most popular games for kids in the neighborhood was a game called stickball, a baseball-type game using a broomstick-like bat, a red ball, sewer covers as home and second base, and parts of cars for first and third. The red ball was thrown underhand and twisted and turned as it left the pitcher's hand to make the ball move to the right or left after it bounced. The kids in this particular neighborhood where Long John lived, a neighborhood filled with six-floor brick apartment buildings and near the subway, played stickball as soon as the season warmed up and until the season got too cold. They'd play it through the spring and into the fall.

Back in the day, the larger neighborhood, which included just about everywhere that sent kids to the local elementary school, was itself divided into smaller neighborhoods. There was Long John's neighborhood next to the subway and Queens Boulevard, named after Queens, the New York City borough. This neighborhood's main rival in sports was the neighborhood near the local elementary school.

Their rivalry in all sports was fierce, but in stickball, it was as hot as the sun on a summer beach day. The teams, one named the Subways for obvious reasons and the Parkways because the elementary school was located above a parkway, had a rivalry filled with teasing and bad blood.

One day, these two teams, in keeping with the importance they gave to their stickball rivalry, pitched in after a particularly close game and bought a trophy at the sporting goods shop on Queens Boulevard and had it engraved "Queens Stickball Champions."

The two teams decided on that hot and muggy late August day that the trophy would go back and forth between whichever team won a special last game of the year, kind of like a World Series.

It didn't occur to them that there might be other teams in Queens who might challenge the assumption that only these two particular teams should compete for being the best in a borough of two million people, but who cared? The two teams just cared about winning that trophy that would each year travel like the Stanley Cup in the National Hockey League to each and every member of the team who won the "World Series."

As one particular year's "World Series" game approached, the Subways felt the expectations for their victory grow. They had lost out on the trophy for the last two years, and if they didn't want this temporary embarrassment to become permanent, a win was a must! The Subways were teased in school, not only by the kids on the Parkways, but also by anyone else who wanted to feel better about themselves at their expense. With the weather already cool and sweaters having replaced T-shirts, the game was quickly approaching. The Subways even scheduled extra practices on early Saturday mornings. Long John was always there. His job? To go and gather the foul balls hit into people's yards.

Finally, the day of the big game arrived—a late Wednesday afternoon in the middle of October. The gray sky was filled with the promise of winter, the leaves turning from green to red and yellow and some even beginning to fall. The light was escaping earlier and earlier from the sky, and the weather became more appropriate for football than for baseball. As the Subways walked home from school, they heard the taunts of their peers: "Three losses in a row, and you're out!"

The street looked good for stickball. Cars for first and third bases were there, not too much traffic, and a couple younger kids had already taken seats on the hoods of the Chevys, Fords, Buicks, and Oldsmobiles that lined the street. Even though the Subways were the home team, the other team was up first. The team that had lost the previous year had to. Larry Cerv, a kid with a vicious curveball, went out to the pitcher's mound.

Long John came up to Mike, the captain, and predictably said, "Can I play?"

"You sit on third base, and don't let it drive away."

Everybody laughed, but Long John dutifully went over and sat on third base.

In the first inning, the Subways scored two runs; the Parkways scored four. The next inning, the Subways scored three; the Parkways, two. Then the Subways scored one; the Parkways, none. Subways, three; Parkways, two. Subways, one; Parkways, four. Subways, two; Parkways, none. Subways, none; Parkways, five. Subways, four; Parkways, none. Subways, two!

With a half-inning to go, the street lights coming on, and a cold autumn night wind blowing through the street, the Subways were ahead by one run. By now, new kids from the local school and the neighborhood were filling the hoods of the cars to watch the end of the game. The Subways were one inning from winning back the trophy. They just had to hold the Parkways in this, the last inning, to *no* runs!

Suddenly, they heard someone whistle. It was not unusual to hear whistles at this time of day. In fact, around 5:30, the neighborhood sounded like an Amazonian rain forest. The whistles were parents calling their kids home for dinner. Everyone could identify each whistle like skilled bird-watchers. They heard one particular whistle, and they knew it meant trouble. The whistle belonged to Jimmy's father, and Jimmy was the Subways' best player, best hitter, and best outfielder. Jimmy's presence was essential if the Subways were going to regain the trophy!

"I got to go," said Jimmy.

"You can't go," Mike replied. "Your father can wait for dinner!"

"My father will eat *me* if I don't come home."

"But, it's our last inning! He'll understand."

"The only thing my father understands is that, when he comes home from work, he's hungry! I got to go."

Now the Subways had to hold the Parkways to no runs without their best player. They would have to secure a win without the only person who could always be counted on to catch a fly ball or to stop a swiftly hit ball from escaping into the far beyond. If by some chance the other team was able to tie the game, the Subways would be without their best hitter. There was no way anyone on the field or watching thought that the Subways were going to win without Jimmy.

Out of the corner of his eye, Mike saw what looked like a scarecrow jumping up and down, up and down. It was tall and skinny Long John with his fingers pointed to his chest as if to say, "Me, me! I can play!" A few of the guys looked at each other and, with a shrug of the shoulder, nonverbally said, "We have no choice."

"OK, Long John, get out there."

Long John Skinny loped like a giraffe into the outfield, smiling ear to ear. Many in the field silently dreaded what would happen if the ball were hit to him.

With tension growing, their first batter hit a single. Their second batter hit a pop fly, easily caught. Their third batter hit another single. The other runner went to third, and now there were runners on first and third. Their fourth batter struck out. Their fifth batter walked. Bases loaded, two outs, the sun going down. A hit would probably score two runs, and they would win.

Jody Arroyo, their best hitter, stood at the plate looking like a walking brick, with muscles rippled like waves in the ocean. They say he hit a ball once that went into orbit, and rumor had it that one time he hit a ball so high the sun got worried. Folks in airplanes reported seeing a stickball pass them while in flight. Someone even once heard a ball that was coming to him at the plate cry out in fright, "Don't hit me!"

Jody Arroyo stared at the pitcher with a look that could make birds fall from the sky. The first pitch was a strike. The second, a ball. The third, a ball. The fourth, a swing and a miss. The fifth, a ball. Now, a full count, bases loaded, a hit would win the game.

"Hit it out to me, Jody! Hit it out to me!"

No one could believe it. There was Long Johnny Skinny, taunting Jody Arroyo to hit the ball out to him! What was he thinking?

"Shut up, Long John!" Mike yelled.

Then the pitch. Jody turned on it, and the ball flew from his bat like a champagne cork being released from a just-shaken bottle. His bat swung so fast that the wind from it could have knocked down a house in China. As bat hit ball, it soared like a cannonball from a cannon, far past any fielder and practically into a new neighborhood, and it just kept traveling like it was a crying runaway kid who never wanted to come home. It soared and soared, and the entire Subway team turned in unhappy acceptance that they had lost yet another title game to their dreaded rivals, when the catcher for the Subways yelled, "Look!"

Everyone in the field turned, and there was Long John Skinny churning those long thin arms and legs like pistons on an Indianapolis 500 car, running as fast as he could out, out, out into the street, past one intersection and a second, until he reached up, grabbed the ball in the air, fell to the ground, and tumbled and rolled and tumbled and rolled and tumbled and rolled, until he got up, raising his hand into the air, and said "I got it!" The Subways won the game, and the team simultaneously and joyously leaped into the air and onto Long John Skinny, as he returned to home plate with that ball tightly wrapped between his long, skinny fingers and face beaming like the sun in mid-July.

From that time on, Long John Skinny played in every game the Subways played and in every sport! It turned out that those long, skinny arms that were made fun of could now play first base and grab balls that would have been thrown too high for anyone else. Those long, skinny arms that he was teased about could now grab football passes that would have been thrown too far for anyone else, and those long, skinny arms that were always the brunt of jokes could now grab rebounds that no one else would have gotten.

Long John Skinny played in every game after that, but from that time on, his name was simply John.

QUESTIONS FOR STUDENTS

- Have you ever known anyone who was teased and not included in the activities of your friends? Tell us about him or her.
- Have you ever been teased and excluded from the games of others? What did you do and how did you feel?
- Have you ever noticed that people sometimes have skills and talents you never realized they had? When did you notice, and what skills did you discover?
- When you were being excluded from certain groups of kids, did you ever wish they could really get to know who you were and what powers and skills you had?
- How do you think we can all we make sure that we take advantage of the skills and talents of all the people around us?
- Why does it feel like you are cool when you can get others to make fun of someone else? Do you feel that this kind of cool cred (if it exists) lasts a long time, or is it short-lived? Why?
- Did laughing at the jokes made at Long John's expense make the other kids equally responsible for making him feel bad? What else could they have done, and why don't you think they did it?

THOUGHTS FOR STUDENTS

The skills and talents that some of the kids I went to school with often surprised me. Whether it was working with someone on a science fair project and realizing how good they were at building, watching the shy girl draw beautifully, noticing how good a bowler a nonathletic kid was, or hearing a seemingly nerdy kid play a mean guitar, it was always eye-, mind-, and heart-opening to realize that my initial judgment of someone was wrong.

Many times, our initial views about people are just that: immediate and based on very partial information and prejudice. Understanding that has kept me from making snap decisions about whether I should exclude someone from my life. It has opened me up to what others can teach me in spite of what I might have thought of someone at first. Long John Skinny, in his own way, was trying to tell his friends that not only could he play ball, but he could also help his team attain its goal. By continually excluding him from games, the Subways were not only hurting him but also themselves.

I still remember this kid who went to my YMCA camp one year and played piano while the rest of us played Ping-Pong and talked about sports. Because it was a sports-oriented camp, his talents were not really appreciated, and he didn't come back to camp the next year. I'll always remember his name because it was two first names. It was the then-not-famous but now internationally known rock star Billy Joel.

There was another kid, this one in my elementary school, who was really smart in science and math but, again, not very good in sports. We really didn't hang with him. His name was Walter Becker, and he went on to start one of the most important rock bands of the 1970s and 1980s: Steely Dan. Another kid in high school had long, stringy hair and was not very friendly. I didn't go out of my way to be friends with him, although I could tell that he was smart. His name was John Cummings; he changed his name to Johnny Ramone and helped to create the great punk band the Ramones.

You never know what talents are living inside people. In a sports-oriented world, those who can play sports well are honored, and those who can't aren't. If we were a culture that depended on hunting for eating, those who were good trackers and marksmen would be honored, while those who couldn't would be considered to have less value.

Often, who is noticed, honored, and considered cool depends on the things you and your friends value. Don't limit yourself that way. Expand what you let yourself notice, what you admire, and who you allow in. The world is much bigger than the territory you and your friends have carved out. Someone who is big can afford to admit that they don't know everything. They can recognize that shutting out someone because that person doesn't fit into an idea of what is cool is limiting the possibility to learn and benefit from them.

Someone who is confident doesn't have to build up their cred by running down someone else. How courageous is it to tackle someone who, for whatever reason, is weaker or not considered cool? Just because you can beat someone in one-on-one who just picked up a basketball for the first time doesn't mean that you're all that. It's also no big deal that you can kick someone when they are down. It gives you a false sense of your own superiority. By picking on the more vulnerable in your circle, you not only close down the chance to learn and benefit from that person, but you also help to create an environment where everyone is always walking on egg shells. A culture of teasing spreads—even to you!

Those who laughed when John was teased are what we call bystanders and are in some ways even more cowardly than the bully. Why? Because the bystander tells him- or herself that they are not really doing anything bad yet; at the same time, they are collecting the rewards of being part of the in group. Bystanders want to be accepted, want to be part of a group, and desperately don't want the teasing turned on them. They fool themselves into thinking that they are not as guilty as those who are committing the acts. By staying back, they help to continue a culture that makes bullying and teasing acceptable, and while they may be temporarily freed from being a target, it does not fully free them in the long run.

Remember, not everyone is good at everything, but everybody is good at something. It is important and beneficial for you to have the confidence to move outside your comfort zone and to realize the limits of what you see as cool are just that—limits that limit you!

THOUGHTS FOR TEACHERS

Curriculum and Pedagogical Suggestions: Multiple Intelligence Theory, Cooperative Learning

Howard Gardner's multiple intelligence theory recognizes that there are many ways people learn. Gardner believes that it is important to encourage a passion for learning by providing many entry points into the acquisition of knowledge: spatial, linguistic, logical-mathematical, bodily-kinesthetic, musical, interpersonal, intrapersonal, and naturalistic. While there has been criticism of some aspects of Gardner's theory and practice, in my opinion, his important contribution to education is something all good teachers intuitively understand: that students learn differently, that they often shine in different areas, and that we need to be careful about making judgments about how smart someone is until we understand the limits of a particular form measurement. How is this important for our work with prosocial character acquisition?

The more you give your students diverse opportunities to show off, the more confident they become, the more respect they get, and the more others feel comfortable about demonstrating skills that at first seem unacceptable. This might be because of gender expectations, cultural priorities, or what gets tested and what does not. Guard dogs do not necessarily patrol Gardner's categories. People's talents are diverse and often bleed from one category to another. Teaching with Gardner's work in mind allows us to embrace our own and others' diverse skills and styles of learning.

Not only should your pedagogy and curriculum be informed by multiple intelligence theory, but also you should create a learning environment that uses those various skills through cooperative learning. When there is a task to do and a group of kids to do it, they need each other for the successful completion of that task. By needing each other, they learn what each of them can contribute to the success of the whole. They learn to be dependent on diverse skills and talents to make their work easier and the results better.

In the 1990s, in a Providence, Rhode Island, inner-city school, I co-created and directed a "Museum in a School" project. The idea was to have classes travel around the building and neighborhood to engender curiosity about the building, a former factory, and its neighborhood, whose history dated to precolonial times. The next task was to cooperatively choose one aspect of what they were curious about to research and then share the results as a museum exhibit. Classes were charged with developing a research strategy, and each class was coupled with an artist who helped the students mold their research into a museum-quality exhibit. Finally, the classes had to speak about their work, becoming essentially museum docents.

This work provided many ways to show off a variety of skills: observing, speaking, writing, organizing, building, measuring, and painting, among other things. While there were and will always be a few students who didn't want to be involved, for the most part, there was a commitment to participate, to learn, to appreciate, and to benefit from the skills of others. Talents never before seen were revealed, challenges were collectively discussed and overcome, and acceptance of even the most eccentric students was accomplished.

Lastly, at that same school, we used a literacy technique called "accountable talk," where rich teacher–student discussions supported the development of student's reasoning and their ability to express it. One of the phrases that was used as part of this classroom dialogue was, "Building on what so-and-so said." This simple yet powerful phrase taught listening and reasoning skills, while demonstrating the social nature of learning. "Building on what so-and-so did and said"—everyone needs each other to grow and to learn, and the more real-life opportunities you can provide for your students to do so, the more prosocial your classrooms will be.

Not only can pedagogical changes support a community in which students recognize each other's talents, but the content of your curriculum can support this, as well. Obviously, for the younger students, the ugly duckling and even Rudolph the Red-Nosed Reindeer are jumping-off points for a discussion about those who start off being uncomfortably different but soon become, as in Rudolph's case, indispensable because of this difference. The ugly duckling becomes beautiful when he finds his proper community. Having grown-ups in your school or in the parent community tell their personal stories of exclusion would, I'm sure, reveal many other situations where they or others they knew were not recognized for talents that they eventually were appreciated for.

There are, of course, many, many biographies of those who failed this or that test and turned out to be geniuses, those who were cut from this or that team and became stars, those who were considered unattractive and became models, those who were not popular and became politicians (wait a minute—that still might mean they are not popular—but you get it). The more your classroom is rich in these types of stories, the more likely it is that your students will wake up to the fact that their initial judgments of others are based on very partial and limited observations and experiences.

What were your experiences in this regard? Please share them with your students. They want and need to hear them—really!

Chapter Three

The Tickle Karate Master

Howard was very smart. He knew all the states and their capitals by the time he was five. He knew how to multiply and divide by his sixth birthday. He knew the names of the different parts of the atom when he was seven, and by the time Howard was eight, he was reading all about the battles in the Civil War. At nine, Howard was a weather freak and could tell you the names of the different kind of clouds and the likelihood of rain on any day in any city.

Yes, Howard was smart, but he was not much of an athlete. Oh sure, he played baseball, but everyone on the team, everyone watching the game, and even the opposing team held their breath when the ball was hit to Howard in right field. It wasn't for lack of trying. Howard played soccer since he was five, baseball since he was six, and now, at the age of twelve, he had even begun to play football. Let's just say he didn't have the same natural abilities in sports as he did for book learning, which of course was quite fine, and to tell you the truth, his lack of ability in sports didn't really bother him at all. Whichever sport Howard played, he played with the same confidence he took into a math or spelling test.

Although not super popular, Howard was sort of just tolerated. Maybe sometimes he was a little more than tolerated, when he answered a particularly difficult social studies question or knew how photosynthesis worked. On these occasions, there were even some kids who were secretly proud that they knew someone as smart as Howard.

But there was one boy in school who didn't like Howard *at all*. For Dante, Howard was the pebble in his shoe, and Dante, unfortunately, was the bully in the school. Dante was about six inches taller than the other kids in his grade and even had just the slightest hint of a mustache growing under his nose in seventh grade. He had muscles under his sleeveless shirts and pants that were always torn by what everyone guessed was some kind of fight or accident he got into doing something dangerous or forbidden.

Dante didn't like Howard, and Howard was just plain scared of Dante. Dante would trip Howard in the hall, steal his lunch money, and use the back of Howard's head like a basketball backboard, bouncing it again and again as he and Howard were waiting in line for the bus. But, what was Howard to do? Dante was about a foot taller and plenty stronger, and Howard felt that, if he told his teacher or his parents, the bullying he'd receive would be much more severe than it already was.

Also, sadly, none of the kids in the school said anything, as well, fearing that Dante would turn on them. It was just one of those things that Howard thought that he would have to tolerate until he either went to another school or, hopefully, grew taller and stronger than Dante.

One Sunday morning, when the rest of his family was still sleeping, Howard went for a walk on the boulevard near his house. He liked Sundays, slower and more quiet than the other days of the week. There were very few cars on the road, stores were still closed, and often he was the only person walking. Howard walked past Mr. Barenberg's candy store, where he always bought and opened his baseball cards while sipping a Cherry Coke and munching on a long, thin pretzel. He passed by M and M grocers, where all food came packaged with a thin layer of dust. And, he walked past Zimmerman's butcher shop.

Then, a surprise: In front of a store that never was rented was a two-dimensional cardboard circus strongman wearing a long, one-piece black-and-white horizontally striped bathing suit, and beneath his muscled legs and feet, seemingly begging for mercy, was someone that looked like an all-grown-up version of Dante!

"If ever I could get Dante beneath my feet, I would be happy forever!" Howard thought.

From a speaker atop the door, suddenly, a deeply booming godlike voice echoed. "Would *you* like to learn an ancient system of self-*defense?*"

Howard looked up at the speaker. "Well yes," he said shyly.

"Then come on *innnnnnn!*" the voice echoed into the otherwise silent Sunday morning.

Howard walked into the store, and the first thing he noticed was how highly polished the wooden floors were and how white the walls were. His eyes rested on a small sign in a glass-covered frame. "Dr. Thaddeus J. Brickrock's School of Self-Defenseology," it said. Then, from a speaker attached to the wall on top of the sign, he heard that same booming voice he had heard outside moments before. "Are you ready to devote your time to learning a system of self-defense that I learned high in the Himalaya Mountains?"

"I am," Howard answered.

"Then assume a fighting position."

Howard complied, yet with his feet extended so far from the rest of his body he almost fell over and with so much room between his arms he could have hugged a refrigerator, his fighting position was as far from a boxer's stance as a frog sitting on a rock.

"Feet and hands closer together," the voice from the speaker erupted.

Howard shifted his feet and hands.

"Fingers out!"

"I wonder which finger he means?" Howard thought.

Scarily, as if the voice could read Howard's mind: "Pointer fingers!"

Howard complied.

"Goooooood! Now, repeat after meeeeeeee: May the farce be with you!" Howard didn't really know what that word meant, but he thought it had something to do with humor, and although he had no clue why this would be part of a martial arts lesson, he nonetheless repeated it, albeit in a softer voice.

"May the farce be with you!"

"Gooooood! Knock, knock!"

"What now?" Howard thought to himself.

"Knock, knock!" called out the voice with a greater sense of urgency.

"Who's there?" answered Howard.

"Ima."

"Ima who?"

"Ima glad you came in here today."

"Where *am* I?" Howard thought to himself.

"Now it's time for your finger exercise," the voice continued.

"In, out, in, out, around! In, out, in, out, around! In, out, in, out, around!"

With each command, Howard threw out his pointer finger and twirled it.

"In, out, in, out, around. In, out, in, out, *around*!"

"Good. Next week come back with chocolate chip cookies to pay me for *lessons*."

The voice simply stopped, leaving the studio silent. Howard walked outside. He considered how weird that guy was but figured that, if this is what he had to do to get Dante beneath his feet, then he would do it!

During the week, during each of Dante's torments, Howard imagined what he would do to Dante after he learned martial arts. As Dante was putting spitballs down the back of his shirt, Howard imagined reaching back, taking Dante by the head, and throwing him onto the teacher's desk. As Dante tripped him in the hall, Howard imagined taking Dante's legs, twisting them into a pretzel, and throwing him into the principal's office.

At the end of this week filled with dreaming and imagining, on Saturday night, Howard asked his parents if they could make some chocolate chip cookies.

"Sure," his mother answered.

"Can we make more than usual?" Howard asked.

"Why?" asked his father.

"Because I really like them," Howard answered.

Even after eating lots of batter and some still-warm cookies, plenty were left.

On Sunday morning, Howard dressed, grabbed the extra cookies, and excitedly went to the boulevard and past the candy store, the grocery store, and the butcher shop, until once again he was in front of the strongman with the Dante look-alike beneath his muscled legs.

Into the store Howard walked, much more confidently than he had been the week before. He put the cookies underneath the speaker, and the familiar voice boomed, "There are not enough chips in those cookies! I like more chocolate chiiiiiiipssssssss!"

"I'm sorry," said Howard, not knowing quite what to do or say and filled with remorse.

"It's all *right*. Get into fighting position."

Howard complied, looking a bit more like a real fighter than he had the week before.

"Good!" yelled the voice. "Did you practice during the week?"

Not wanting to get into more trouble than he already had, Howard hesitantly said, "Yes."

"*Liar!*" the voice bellowed, almost knocking Howard to the floor.

"You're right," said Howard sheepishly.

"Say it!"

"May the farce be with you," replied Howard, still smarting from the shock of the loud admonition.

"Gooooodddddd! Knock, knock."

"Who's there?"

"Orson."

"Orson, who?"

"Stop Orson around, and let's get on with the lesson!"

Having a knock-knock joke at the beginning of a martial arts session seemed odd to Howard, and he couldn't hold back from asking, "What does this knock-knock joke have to do with this martial art?"

"Just *do* it!" replied the voice, leaving no room for questions or debate. "Fingers extended. In, out, in, out, around. In, out, in, out, around. In, out, in, out, around. In, out, in, out, around. In, out, in, out, around. And a new direction: left, out, right, out, around. Left, out, right, out, around!"

Howard threw out arm after arm, and at the end, out went his pointer finger, and it twisted like a corkscrew.

"In, out, in, out, around. In, out, in, out, around. Left thrust, around. Right thrust, around," the disembodied voice called out. Suddenly and shockingly, a belt dropped and dangled from the ceiling. It was yellow, and it had *pink* polka dots!

The voice continued, "This is your first belt in the great march of belts in the self-defense system you are learning. If you work hard, one day you will attain the ultimate belt, the purple belt with the ten thousand *smiiiiles!*" The last word echoed against the studio's walls.

"Now take this belt, wrap it around your waist, and return next week, having practiced and with chocolate chip cookies with more *chiiiiiiiippppppppssss!*"

Howard walked out onto the street; felt the cold, crisp, early-winter air; and wrapped the belt around his waist. He felt a jolt of confidence, like a bolt of lightning running through his body. He practiced his exercises: left, out, right, out, around. Left, out, right, out, around. He felt his confidence grow with each step he took. By the time Howard was home, his head was so drunk with confidence that he knew on Monday he had one thing to do: He was finally going to challenge Dante to a *fight*!

On Monday, Howard walked out his apartment building door and wrapped the long yellow belt with pink polka dots around his waist. As he walked, he did his exercises. Left, out, right, out, around. He was heading for a *showdown*! As Howard approached the schoolyard, he immediately noticed Dante leaning against the chain-link schoolyard fence, surrounded by the other cool guys in the school. Howard stopped about one foot away and got into the position he had learned at the studio; feet spread, hands extended, with the pointer finger displayed.

Dante and his friends looked quizzically in his direction. "OK, Dante," Howard said in a voice that was higher pitched than usual. "OK, Dante," Howard repeated. "I'm sick and tired of being picked on by you. *Sick and tired.* Did you hear me? *Sick and tired*! You're in big trouble, Dante. *Big* trouble."

"OK, Dante. May the farce be with you."

Dante just held his gaze with a cynical smile on his lips. "OK, Dante. Knock, knock." Dante just stared, as did the cool guys who surrounded Dante like bodyguards. "I said, 'Knock, knock!'" Howard became more and more frustrated when no answer was forthcoming. "I *said*, 'Knock, knock!'" emphasizing the word *said* as if he was a teacher trying to control the class.

"OK, Dante. OK, Dante. You got to three to say 'Who's there?' or I'm coming to get you!"

"One," Howard said, letting the word roll from his mouth.

"OK, Twooooooooo! Dante, I'm like a pot of water about to boil over. Two and a haaaaaaalf. I'm like a balloon ready to pop. Two and threeee-quarterrrrrrrrssssss. I'm like a firecracker about to explode. Two and seven-eighths. That's bigger than two and three-quarters, in case you don't know that, stupid Dante, who failed the last two math tests. He failed the last two math tests. Hey everybody," Howard chanted, with his confidence building, repeating that sentence like thunder rolling through the sky in a storm. "He failed the last two math tests. He failed the last two math tests. He failed the last two math tests." And then suddenly, "Three!" jumped from Howard's mouth and toward Dante and into the crowd that had formed, completely hypnotized by the amazing scene unfolding in front of them.

When Dante didn't respond, Howard's finger went toward Dante and at the same time, Dante's left arm came out like a jack-in-the-box and landed right in the middle of Howard's face. Dante's arm was so long that Howard couldn't even touch him. Those arms just flailed like a rope in the wind. Dante held back Howard until he was tired of doing so and then reached back his right arm and—boom!—landed a fist on Howard's eye!

When Howard awoke, he was in the nurse's office, lying on one of those hard cots and surrounded by eye charts and medicine cabinets. There was something cold on his eye. It was an ice pack. He took the now-dripping ice pack off his eye, looked in the mirror, and there it was: a black eye. A big black eye!

As you can imagine, the next six days were not the best in Howard's life. Some laughed as he came down the halls; others giggled. His parents demanded an explanation, but through it all, Howard maintained his silence. He walked straight ahead in the halls at school, noticing no one. He lied to his parents. He fumed silently about how Dr. Brickrock had failed him, and he couldn't wait until Sunday to tell him so. When Sunday finally arrived, Howard decided that he would hold back his anger for a while. Perhaps he did not want to be rude, or perhaps, when it came down to it, he was kind of shy in the studio where the voice filled up all the empty space. As he put the cookies down as payment, the voice bellowed, "What happened to youuuuu?"

"I bumped into a pole," Howard, shyly yet with a tinge of anger, answered.

"Liarrrrrr!" the voice retorted. With that, Howard's anger and pain poured out.

"Yeah, you're right. I got hit. Hit! Your stupid martial art didn't work. I challenged Dante to a fight, and look what happened!"

A thick moment of silence greeted Howard's explosion. Then suddenly, "Who told you to start a fight? You are learning a system of self-*de*fense, not *off*ense. You are supposed to *stop* fights, not *start* them. Besides, you need to learn how to learn, one step at a time. And all that you've had were two lessons in the art of tickle karateeeee!"

It took these words about two seconds to soak into Howard's head. Tickle karate?

"Tickle karate?"

"Yes, *tickle karate*," came the voice. "Now, get into position to learn."

Each week for months after, Howard learned each tickle karate position with the discipline he had for learning about science, math, history, or anything else, for that matter. He learned the points on the body that are particularly ticklish, the positions' names, and the names of famous old-time movie comedians. There was the "Groucho Marx point" under the arms, the "Charlie Chaplin point" on the left side of the belly, the "Buster Keaton point" on right side of the belly. Each of the points had a new belt: the red belt with the green birthday cakes, the golden belt with the silver bowling balls, and the black belt with the white parking meters.

Each week, Howard returned and learned with the predictability and discipline of a minute hand circling the numbers on a clock. After many months of hard work, Howard was one belt away from the ultimate belt: the purple belt with the ten thousand smiles.

It was the last day of school, a hot and muggy day. It was the type of June day in New York City when sweat pours off of your body even if you are not walking, the kind of day that speaks of summer even if the calendar says that you are still in the last days of spring. It was this kind of day, the last day of school, when Howard cleaned out his locker and threw away old tests, PTA letters never delivered to his parents ("Oh, that's where it went!"), and a few broken pencils and crayons. Howard put the books that were still needed under his arm, closed the locker door, and walked through the asphalt schoolyard that seemed to breathe heat in the hot sun.

As he walked through the yard, feeling the heat from the asphalt through his sneakers and not particularly sad to be finished with the most difficult year of his school career, Howard felt someone push the books from under his arm. He reached down for them and realized that a foot was on his math textbook. He followed that foot with his up to the knee, to the chest, to the neck, to the face of—Dante! Dante stood over him like a marble statue on a pedestal. Dante, his bully! Dante, who had made his life miserable all year! Dante!

"Ah, excuse me, Dante, but you're standing on my books."

"Oh really?" answered Dante sarcastically, slowly moving his hands into a fighting position.

"Yeah," said Howard cautiously. "Can I have my books?"

"No," answered Dante ominously.

"But I need my books to go home!" Howard said apologetically.

"And I need to give you a little present to make sure that you remember me all summer," said Dante.

"That's not a problem, Dante. I have a good memory, and you are a very memorable fellow."

"Let's go," said Dante, his fists out like the heads of two poisonous snakes ready to strike.

"No, I don't like fighting," said Howard to Dante, as well as to the entire school population, who were drawn to the smell of a schoolyard fight.

"Come on," said Dante.

"No, I don't like to fight."

"Scared, aren't you?" said Dante, dripping with scorn.

"No, I just don't like fighting."

"Let's go," said Dante with the inevitability of a thick, gray sky filled with dark clouds. "Let's go!" he repeated, growing ever more frustrated by Howard's unwillingness to engage and to allow Dante a final pleasure he so sincerely and clearly sought on this, the last day of school. "Let's go!"

Howard's legs slowly spread, and his arms extended. His fingers pointed, and he quietly said, "May the farce be with you. Knock, knock."

"OK. Who's there?" said Dante, willing to indulge Howard in this game almost as if he was a prison warden granting a final meal to a prisoner on death row.

"Duane," answered Howard.

"Duane who?" Dante said quickly.

"Duane the bathtub," said Howard. "I'm dwowning!"

Well that was a good one, and Dante couldn't resist a little chuckle, laughing as much about Howard's nerdiness as from power of the joke. But, as Dante laughed, Howard realized that Dante had his arms down and was momentarily vulnerable, so he quickly went on the attack: A left pointer finger under Dante's arm, a right under the other arm, another left to Dante's belly, and still another one to the right arm. Left, right, left, right, around. Left, right, left, right, around. The fingers poked into each tickle point on Dante's body. Left, right, left, right, around. Left, right, left, right, around.

Dante laughed so hard that he was soon on the ground, while Howard continued his relentless attack. Left, right, left, right, around. Left, right, left, right, around. Dante writhed with laughter and pain.

"Stop!" he yelled. "What are you doing? I can't breathe. I can't breathe. Stop! Stop! OK, already. I give!"

A silenced schoolyard had just witnessed the previously unthinkable: the all-powerful Dante rendered helpless under the mighty fingers of Howard!

"Stop! I quit!"

Those words soared to the heavens like doves. Unexpected words. Words as powerful as "Let there be light" or "The Giants win the pennant" or "Ask not what your country can do for you but what you can do for your country." Words that changed the world of these students as surely as Neil Armstrong's "one small step for man, one giant step for mankind" changed the world for those in that time. With those words, certainty had ended, and the bully was finally defeated—not by a punch but by a tickle. Howard blew on both fingers and put them in his pockets with the flare of a cowboy whose guns just won a duel with a bandit. He picked up his books and walked through the schoolyard.

First one voice and then another and then another called out, "Hey, Howard! Let's get together this summer."

"Nice job, Howard!"

"Howard, what are you doing tomorrow?"

Howard turned to his now-adoring fans, snapped his fingers, and coolly said, "We'll see!"

Once out of the hot blacktop schoolyard, Howard heard someone running behind him. He turned, and as you might have guessed, it was Dante! He nervously thought he'd have to fight one more time, but instead, Dante, still trying to get his hair in place and his dignity back, said, "Hey, Howard, that's quite a martial art you learned. Maybe you can teach it to me in September."

Howard looked at his old nemesis and simply said, "Do you have a phone, Dante?"

"Sure," he answered.

"Give me a call, and we'll talk." Howard turned and walked home.

The following Sunday, as he walked toward the storefront, he noticed for the first time in months that there was no cardboard cutout in front of the store. All that was there was a note on a door with his name on it and an envelope below. He quickly read the note:

Dear Howard,

You have learned tickle karate better than anyone I've ever taught. Now it is time for me to leave and to teach others and for you to teach all those locally with a desire to learn. Below is an envelope with some gifts for you.

Howard opened the envelope. The first thing that caught his eye was a piece of paper, an official certificate, like the kind that used to be on the wall of the studio or the kind that was found in the doctor's office. It said, "Degree in Tickle Karate, Dr. Thaddeus J. Brickrock's School of Self-Defenseology." Then, as he reached his hand further down into the envelope, there it was: the belt—*the purple belt with the ten thousand smiles*!

Howard took the belt, wrapped it around his waist, and walked home, never again to be bothered by Dante, the bully.

QUESTIONS FOR STUDENTS

- Have you ever been bullied or teased? If so, what happened, and how did it feel?
- Have you ever bullied someone? What did you do, and why do you think you did it? Did it make you feel good?

- If you bullied someone, did you notice how the person you bullied felt? If so, what did you notice? How did that make you feel?
- Why do you think people are bullies?
- In this story, how did the other kids react to Dante's bullying of Howard? Could they have reacted differently? If so, how?
- How have you reacted when you've seen someone being picked on?
- If you stood by and watched, how did that make you feel?
- Can you think of another way you could have behaved that would have made you feel better?
- What do you think were Howard's options when he realized that he was being bullied? Why didn't he take them?
- What was the tickle karate master trying to teach Howard about the use of violence to fight violence?
- Have you ever used violence to stop violence? If so, was it successful?
- If someone, yourself included, were being bullied, what would you suggest they do?

THOUGHTS FOR STUDENTS

In some ways, this story is unrealistic in that tickle karate can't really be used to stop a bully, but through this story, I make a point. When Howard tried to use violence to stop violence, he was unable to do so. Dante was stronger, and he wasn't about to be defeated by someone who everyone knew was physically weaker. However, when Howard was creative, using an unexpected tactic to fight Dante, the results were better. When Howard tried to show how cool he was using his newly obtained martial art, he was defeated, but when he let Dante's aggressive energy turn against himself, Howard was victorious.

While using humor to defuse potentially difficult situations is not always successful, it is a good idea to try. Laughter often acts as glue between people, creating a bond while releasing anger. It is difficult to fight when you are laughing. It is difficult to dislike someone when you share one of those laughs you can't stop. If not humor, though, to stop a bully, creativity is needed.

You will not always have tickle karate to help you deal with the difficult situation of being bullied, but you do have your mind and your observational skills, and because of that, you will have many options short of resorting to violence to stop a bully's behavior.

If, however, your humor, friendliness, or sincerity do not work, you have a right and indeed an obligation to tell an adult and to ask for protection. Bullying is a very serious matter. Kids who are bullied often don't want to go to school for fear of being attacked. It affects their schoolwork and can make them sick. No one has the right to be put into that kind of position, where their education, health, and mental well-being are in jeopardy.

Bullying does not just happen on the schoolyard or in the classroom either. Bullying doesn't always involve physicality. Aggressive teasing, teasing where one person or more continues to make fun, sometimes with the threat of physical violence in the background, is bullying, too. So is teasing over the Internet on Facebook or Twitter, for that matter. Whenever one or more people gang up on another person in an attempt to make to make that person feel bad about themselves and make themselves feel superior, it is bullying, even if a punch is never thrown.

Remember, there is nothing wrong and everything right about admitting to a grown-up that you are overwhelmed by somebody's behavior. We all have been in that position, where, for some reason or another, a kid just doesn't like you and decides to advance their status by bullying. It doesn't reflect badly on you or indicate weakness to admit that a situation is too great for you to handle on your own. In fact, to be able to admit your vulnerability indicates strength.

Tell someone, and don't let it continue! If someone is bullying you, there is a good chance that he or she has bullied someone else and that they will do so in the future. By calling attention to the bullying, you might be saving others the hardship that you are feeling.

Who is the bully, and why does he or she do what they do? Well, there are probably a lot of different types of people and a lot of different reasons for those who become bullies. Sometimes it's someone who his being physically harmed at home. Not only is he or she carrying around a great deal of unhappiness, but also the culture of their home is not permitting them to deal with their sadness through conversation or caring.

Violence is often a way that someone who feels powerless can momentarily feel powerful. Those who bully are often insecure themselves and use bullying as a way to increase their social status. Sometimes they haven't felt the joy of working together with others and only know how to increase their self-esteem by making someone else feel bad. Sometimes bullies are not terribly good at school or sports and are unable to get attention any way else.

For whatever reason people choose to bully, two things are clear: (1) Bullying never really gets you what you need, and (2) it must stop because no one has a right to bring pain to another person or make another person insecure.

If you consider yourself a bully, I would suggest that you find a counselor, a teacher, or a parent and talk with them about how you often resort to violence when you feel angry or sad or want to be noticed. None of these are valid reasons to hurt anyone psychologically or physically, and this kind of behavior will not only get you in trouble and make your life more difficult but also will not get you what you need. Speak with a grown-up! They've often been in the same position you're in, unable to control their urge to bully. They *want* to help. Give them a chance. You really have no healthy alternative, and remember, there is no harm in admitting that you need help. None!

The last actors in this story are those in the school who watched and often laughed at Dante's bullying of Howard. By providing a supportive audience for Dante, these bystanders gave their approval for Dante's actions. Because bullies often want and thrive off attention, you are giving them just what they think they need, and you are encouraging their behavior by doing so.

By standing by, seemingly passively, you are giving the bully fertile soil for his or her actions. While others are looking and not saying anything, bullies not only feel empowered to continue but also feel that, if they stop, they will lose face in front of those looking on. Watching and sometimes laughing along with a bully's action is called bystander behavior. This be-havior is not passive or neutral, meaning that you can't pretend that you are not involved. You are, and you know it!

How many of you have watched someone bullied and have felt bad be-cause you have seen another person suffer? Of course, you and all of us have. We are hardwired to be compassionate human beings and to empathize or to feel another's pain. When we stand by and watch bullying occur, we are fighting these natural qualities of compassion in ourselves out of the fear of sticking out, being a goody-goody, and becoming a target ourselves and are left feeling empty and guilty.

Remember, watching is participating. As surely as people in a play need an audience to be actors, the bully needs passive bystanders. You are giving approval to the bully by not saying anything, and remember, there are often more people who don't like what the bully is doing than those who do. Although it's difficult to do so, stick up for what you know is right. Say something to the bully, to others around you, to an adult. You'll feel better that you do, guaranteed!

THOUGHTS FOR TEACHERS

Curriculum and Pedagogical Suggestions: History and Economic Policy

You are all aware of the harm bullying can cause. You've seen it in your classrooms, your homes, in your childhood. Having been bullied or having been a bully in the past and having now grown up to assume your adult roles in your job, family, and community, you might by now have brushed those experiences off, thinking they were things that kids had to endure on their way to becoming an adult. Please do not think that. Not only is the pain of being bullied excruciating and the isolation wrenching, but also being bullied often leaves psychological scars that linger through one's life.

A man, now in his late sixties, recently related a story of how, when he was fourteen, he had been somewhat of a bully. He came from a house where there had been a lot of anger and frustration. Recently, he went on Facebook, and he quickly received two friend requests by people whose names he sort of remembered. He accepted the friend requests, and it wasn't long before each person wrote back and told him how miserable he had made their lives, fifty or so years after the incidents had happened and with the boys now men of more than sixty!

There is nothing natural or inevitable about bullying or aggressive teasing, whether it is in the street or on Facebook. Is it too often part of growing up? Sure. Will some of it always be with us? Probably. But, so will gun violence and so will slavery and so will people dying because they don't have enough food or medicine. But, that doesn't allow us to close our eyes and walk away from the abuse of power wherever it happens. Bullying is aggressively using one's power to intimidate another for the purposes of exploitation.

When a bully bullies, he or she is hoping to get something out of that relationship, be it a social advantage or simply a way to deal with the anger in their lives. As we allow it to happen, not only are we hurting the one being bullied, but we are also creating false hope for the bully, who somehow believes that his or her social stature will be advanced and their inner demons conquered by his or her act of aggression. Not addressing the bystander is also fostering illusion, the illusion that the bystander can be unaffected by their nonactions.

How can you address these issues, helping your students understand that bullying is part of a larger power dynamic in our society, one that leaves lasting scars and that doesn't ultimately deliver what it promises, and that very few are happy living in a culture that allows unequal power relationships to escalate to the point of bullying?

First, there must be an atmosphere in your classroom conducive to speaking openly about this, as well as other personal issues. Reading books about bullying and bystander behavior and discussing them is a good place to start. These discussions can and should lead to discussion about how bullying has affected your students and you personally. Make sure that everyone in the triad of bullying—the bully, the bullied, and the bystander—gets to speak. Many students have experienced all three of these roles. Use these articulated experiences to accomplish three things:

1. To notice how a culture of bullying affects everybody and how it makes everyone feel.

2. To recognize how other behavioral choices could have made things better. For instance, have the bully talk about what would have made him or her stop bullying. Ask the bullied how others could have made him or her feel better while he or she was in the throes of being bullied. Find out from the bystanders what would have supported their involvement in stopping the violence they were effectively sanctioning by their supposed passivity.

3. To collectively create a policy for dealing with bullying and harassment in your classroom and school. Discuss and decide what will be addressed and how. How will students agree to act when they see bullying or harassment? Can all students agree to say something without the fear of retribution or being labeled a tattletale or a snitch? How do they want adults to be involved? How are bullies to be treated?

Remember, by building on your own and your student's experiences and by helping students take responsibility for their culture, you empower students to be proactive and to take the first steps toward creating the world they want to inhabit. Not a bad civics lesson to teach students that they have control over the world they will be part of.

The final component in helping students become aware of the power imbalance of bullying and harassment is by studying how bullying not only happens in the schoolyard but also happens between nations and within different sectors of any country. Look at how the United States has dealt with the power imbalances that come from monetary or vocational status discrepancies, racism, and sexism.

Our country's political system of checks and balances is a good place to start. The founding fathers' commitment to shared governing led to a system where one branch of government watches over another. Studying how this was set up and how it did or didn't work through different time periods is a good way to bring American history into your discussions about power imbalances and how to rectify it.

There were times in America's history, such as now, when corporate or money power threatened to control the government and how it allocated rights, privileges, and opportunities. How has the United States dealt or not dealt with that? Which kind of regulatory systems are set up? What protections have been removed? Which kinds of tax systems have been chosen at various points in history to foster or not foster equality? Which laws about lobbying have been set up or removed to thwart the influence of money on the creation of laws and codes? Which opportunities have been afforded to educate or to provide jobs for those whose families are not wealthy, so that those people and their children can have an opportunity to not only make their own lives better but others' lives, as well?

How has the United States created opportunities or not created them for newly arrived immigrants? How has or hasn't the United States tried to rectify the power imbalances that came from America's treatment and violent conquest of its native populations, slavery, racism, and sexism? Which role have unions played in equalizing power relationships between those who own places of employment and those who are employed there?

How has the power of unionism changed over the decades? Did the U.S. government ever act in a way that supported or didn't support the creation of unions? Does the United States do all it can to make voting easy, and if not, what else can it do? Finally, how has everyone benefited when our country tried to equalize power and opportunity?

In New York City in the 1920s and 1930s, my father's immigrant family was very poor and took in laundry to wash and iron to earn money. Luckily, the four brothers in the family were able to attend college in the New York City college system for free. Three of the four brothers became lawyers, and one became an accountant. Think of all the tax money they put back into the system. Here is an example of how intelligently equalizing a power imbalance helped everybody. Think of this when you are helping your students with bullying and harassment.

An intelligent solution to bullying or harassment is not only admonition but also a solution that creates a win-win for everyone! No one wins when bullying and power imbalances are the rule. No one really gets what they need, not even bullies or the wealthy. Bullies never solve their deeper issues by bullying, and the wealthy, like it or not, have to deal with the consequence of letting inequality fester.

Chapter Four

How Important Is a House of Cards?

Chloe built a first floor. Chloe built a second floor, and her younger brother, John would say, "How 'bout a third floor?" Chloe would reply, "It's not strong enough." John would say, "Uh huh!" Chloe would say, "Nuh uh!" and John, "Uh huh!"

"Nuh uh!"

Then John would say "Ask Mom, she's right behind you." Chloe would look around for her mother. "Ma! Ma! Ma!" she'd scream and when she turned around, John would be putting a third floor on when the whole thing fell!

One morning, Chloe woke up to the sound of a wolf howling into the second-floor window of the six-floor red brick apartment building that she lived in in New York City. She thought, "A wolf, right here in New York City? I have to see that!" She ran to the window and discovered that it wasn't a wolf but the wind that was blowing and making the panes of glass shutter. A blizzard of snow drifted as high as her second-floor window in patterns that looked like waves at the ocean.

As she stared out the window, hypnotized by the sound of the wind and the sight of the snow, her mother entered the room. "No school today! It's a snow day!"

Chloe and John jumped four feet into the air. "Yes!" they shouted as they ran to the kitchen and took out their overly colored, overly sugared breakfast cereal. The joy was short-lived, cut short by one of their usual fights, this one about who had to return the cereal to the cupboard, with the last one touching the box responsible for putting it away.

"You touched it last!"

"No, you touched it last!"

"No, you touched it last!"

"Hey, look," Chloe said. "There's a prize in the box." John picked up the box to look for the prize. "Got you," Chloe said triumphantly. "You touched it!"

Then, with pieces of fluffy white bread in their hands, Chloe and John went into the living room, turned on cartoons, and rolled the bread into golf-ball-sized balls before putting them in their mouths. The cartoons soon gave way to game shows and reruns of TV comedies, and then came the soap operas. Their mother, cleaning up from the mess Chloe and John had made, realized that her children were captives of a TV-induced hypnotic state and said, "Go into your room and play."

And they did, with their cards.

Chloe built a first floor. Chloe built a second floor, and John said, "How 'bout a third floor?"

"It's not strong enough!" Chloe answered.

"Uh huh," John said.

"Nuh uh," Chloe answered.

"Uh huh," John said.

"Nuh uh," Chloe answered.

"Ask Ma," John said. "She's right behind you."

Chloe turned to ask her mother, but she was not behind her as John had promised. As Chloe turned back toward her brother, she saw that John was putting another card on their stack, attempting to create a third floor—and the whole thing fell!

Frustrated that her younger brother had reversed all of her hard work, she reached back her arm, made a fist, and was just about to hit her brother when their mother entered and said, "Why don't you both go out sledding?"

So, they put on their jackets with the gloves attached, hats with earmuffs, pants with yellow ducks on the red flannel inside, and boots up to their knees and dragged their wooden sleds out the door, down the elevator, and out of the apartment building into snow that was nearly up to their waists. They dragged their sleds to what the neighborhood kids considered one of the highest mountains in the world (it was really only as high as a short eight-year-old boy).

With all the snow, it was difficult to drag the sleds to the top of the hill, so John and Chloe left their sleds at the bottom, walked up the hill, and rolled down. They continued for about an hour, up the hill and down the hill, until the snow was in every part of their clothes and bodies and they were cold and decided to go inside. They dragged their sleds into the building, through the basement, and up the elevator and left them outside their apartment. They knocked on the door, and there was their mother, standing before them with two cups of hot chocolate with little islands of marshmallows floating to the top.

The kids removed their wet clothes, put on dry clothes, and once again played with those cards.

Chloe built a first floor, a second floor, and then carefully—oh so carefully—built a third floor, and John said, "Let's build a fourth floor!"

"It's not strong enough!"

"Uh huh!"

"Nuh uh!"

"Uh huh!"

"Nuh uh!"

"Ask Ma. She's right behind you."

Chloe turned to her mother to proudly tell her how high she had built the house, when once again she realized she had been tricked. Her mother, of course, wasn't behind them, and Chloe turned around in time to see the whole thing fall under the weight of another card.

"That's it," Chloe thought. "My brother is going to get the beating of his life!" She reached back to hit her brother—and there was her mother. "Why don't you build a snowman?"

With reluctance, Chloe went out with John into the front of the building and, with her brother's help, rolled together a ball of snow for the bottom of the snowman, a second slightly smaller ball of snow for the stomach, and then a third for the head. Chloe looked admiringly at their creation. "Where is the neck?"

"Snowmen don't have necks!"

"Oh yeah? How else do you think they eat, stupid?"

"Snowmen don't eat!"

"Uh huh!"

"Nuh uh!"

"Uh huh!"

"Nuh uh!"

"Uh huh!"

"Nuh uh!"

"Ask Mom. She is right behind you, going shopping."

Chloe turned to ask her mother if snowmen ate and of course, once she did, realized that she had again been fooled by her younger brother, but it was too late. As she looked back, she saw her brother putting a neck between the snowman's belly and head and within seconds watched all her efforts at building a perfect snowman fall victim, once again, to her brother. Chloe grabbed a handful of snow, formed it into a snowball, and threw it at her brother. Like a machine gun, she kept taking more and more snow and doing the same. Whack! Whack! Whack!

Chloe left him there, completely covered with snow and went upstairs.

"Where is John?" his mother asked.

"He's playing in the snow."

"Can you go get him? It's time for lunch."

As you can imagine, that was about the last thing Chloe wanted to do, so she took her time. She procrastinated.

She helped Gene, the doorman, put in a lightbulb in the lobby by holding a ladder in place. She went to her friend Stacy's apartment and ate cookies that her grandmother had just taken from the oven. She went down to the basement into the bicycle room to check on her bike, which lay there like a bear in hibernation amid the cobwebs and the dust that had accumulated over the winter, and then, only when she finally felt like it, did she go outside to look for her brother.

But, her brother even made this simple task difficult. She walked around the building ten times, yelling her brother's name. "John! John! John!"

Chloe stopped where she and her brother had been building the snowman, and there, to her surprise, was a snowman, completely built and staring at her with rock eyes. It had a round bottom, a round stomach, a head—and a neck! It had her brother's hat with earmuffs on its head and sticks for arms with her brother's gloves for hands, and she suddenly was filled with a horrible thought!

"I think I've turned my brother into a snowman!"

She frantically began to dig into the snowman's stomach, hoping she would find her brother somehow inside, but she only found more snow.

"I *have* turned my brother into a snowman!" Chloe thought.

Her first instinct was to run away from home, but she realized she was hungry and that she needed to eat before beginning such a long adventure. Her next thought was that there was a chance, slight of course, that her mother would forget she had a son. With that last bit of flimsy hope, she went upstairs, and to her surprise, her mother never even mentioned her brother. Chloe imagined that, yes, her brother had left her mother's mind, hopefully for good. But then, her mother gave Chloe some alphabet soup and the letters slowly spelled out her brother's name: J-O-H-N! Chloe almost knocked the bowl of soup off the table, jumbling the letters in the bowl.

"Chloe, what *are* you doing?"

"Cooling the soup with my spoon," she answered.

Chloe finished her lunch. She began to relax with the thought that, indeed, her brother was forgotten and joyfully ran into her room and yelled, "I got rid of my brother! I got rid of my brother!" She started to plan how she would change the room now that it was all hers, when suddenly the sound of a police siren changed her mood. She realized immediately what had happened. Somehow her mother found out that she had turned her son into a snowman. She called the police, and they were coming to arrest her and put her in jail!

She packed what she imagined she would need for prison: a baseball glove, comics and crayons, her diary, and a biography of Lebron James (her favorite basketball player).

"Mom!" she yelled. "Do you know if they have toothpaste in jail?"

"Chloe," her mother yelled back, "what a strange question. Why are you interested?"

Chloe thought to herself, "You know why!"

She finished packing and looked out the window so that she wouldn't be surprised by the police. Instead of the police, however, she saw the sun, and it was yellow and warm, and it melted the snow on the roof. The water, like a waterfall, spilled down on the window. A thought mixed with happiness and fear entered her brain: "Maybe once the snowman melted, underneath would certainly be John!"

Chloe put on her jacket and ran down the stairs and outside to where her brother was, but instead of seeing her brother, all she saw was a giant puddle with her brother's little hat and gloves floating to the surface. "I turned my brother into a puddle of water!" she cried. "If he ever came back, I'd never yell at him again! He could build the cards as high as he wanted."

"Chloe! Chloe! Chloe!" It was an all-too-familiar voice. John was walking toward her, hand in hand with their beloved grandmother. "I had lunch with Grandma, and you didn't! She gave me two desserts, and you had none! She gave me candy," he said, raising his hand out to show her the candy, "and you can't have any!"

Chloe was seething. She felt like she was about to burst. She felt like taking her brother's head, twisting it off his neck, and kicking it down the street like a football. However, she caught herself, remembering how badly she felt when she thought her brother was a puddle, and slowly counted, "One . . . two . . . three," and took a deep breath and said, "Hi, John. Do you want to play with me?"

"You want me to play with you?" John asked.

Chloe nodded yes.

Chloe and John went upstairs and played with the cards and built the largest first floor they had ever built. A second, as large as that. A third, fourth, and even a fifth floor. John silently looked at their creation and in a voice that meant doom: "How 'bout a sixth floor?"

Chloe couldn't believe what he just said. There was no way what had already been made could ever, ever, hold another floor.

"It's not strong enough," Chloe said.

"Uh huh!"

"Nuh uh!"

"Uh huh!"

"Nuh uh!"

"Ask Mom. She's right behind you."

Chloe turned. "Ma, look how I high I—." But, of course, she wasn't there.

As Chloe turned back, there he was, John with a card in hand, and before she could say anything, that card became, of course, "the straw that broke the camel's back," and the whole thing fell!

At that moment, Chloe wasn't sure whether she would rather have her brother next to her playing cards or downstairs in front of the house as a giant puddle, with his hat and gloves floating to the surface.

QUESTIONS FOR STUDENTS

- Did you ever love and hate the same person within a few seconds of each emotion? When?
- Have you ever said or done something to someone that you regretted later? What was it?
- How could you have stopped yourself from saying or doing something you regretted?
- How is it possible to have conflicting feelings about the same person?

THOUGHTS FOR STUDENTS

Siblings are, in some ways, really good guinea pigs for your future life with others. Emotions with your brothers or sisters can get very heated, yet most of the time you need and indeed care for each other. Your siblings can be the most annoying people in the world, and yet they are, more often than not, there when you need them. You can love and hate them in the time it takes you to blink your eyes.

Our emotions are sly tricksters. They play us like musical instruments, demanding that we pay attention to them as they manipulate us like puppets, provoking our anger and encouraging us to yell and scream to their own amusement. Sometimes I imagine that we are on a stage and everybody's emotions are sitting in the audience, watching us lose our tempers and fume about this slight or that.

Being puppets on strings, being played by our emotions, leaves us without power. We are allowing our emotions to control us rather than the other way around. Emotions want us to act from only short-term vision. They seduce you into feeling justified in acting in a way that you will, more often than not, regret.

The question, of course, is how to control your emotions and not let them control you. Easier said than done. How do you not immediately lash out at someone who, for instance, you feel has pushed you in the hall (as I've done)? How do you not charge at someone whom you feel disrespected by with words or actions (as I've done)? How do you not pay someone back for a perceived slight (OK, that, too)? But, perhaps the better and more important question is, How do you get what you want long term from a situation and not settle for short-term or false victories? I have to admit, I haven't fully figured it out, but I'm trying, and here are some thoughts.

For one, you have to see your emotions as if they are clouds in the sky: they come, and they go. To look up in the sky one day and see that the sun is covered by a thick, gray cloud and to declare that the weather is always awful would be a mistake. Within a minute or so, the clouds could clear, and the sky would open, and the weather would no longer be how you imagined it forever.

Emotions create temporary and partial truths. Anger, jealousy, and resentfulness don't stay forever. It is often the immediate reaction to a perceived slight or the result of lack of sleep, good food, or exercise. A slight one day might not affect you the same way the next. Moods layer on each other, and a perceived slight while you're in a bad mood caused by some social or personal disappointment will seem worse than if that slight happens when you are just back from the beach, just got a kiss from someone you like, or just returned from a game where you scored the winning goal.

To stop yourself from being bossed around by your emotions, you first have to notice that your emotions are trying to control you. Every religion, every philosophy about a good life, begins at the same place: know yourself. When the puppeteer is pulling your strings, when the clouds are temporarily blocking your vision, you have to realize it.

How can we create this kind of smarts? People have dealt with this question forever. I have dealt with this forever. Some people meditate. They sit for five to thirty minutes a day and just watch their breath go in and out. When they have thoughts, they notice them as if they are clouds and just let them go. Don't worry about them. They will pass. Some people exercise or do yoga or tai chi, take walks at the beach, or swim or run long distances. It doesn't matter, as long as we build up our emotion detectors and our ability to let go of the emotions that will lead us on a detour from where we are trying to go: long-term happiness and well-being.

Once this sensitivity seeps into you and you are able to see and feel when you are losing control, how do your stop yourself from becoming a puppet? As difficult as it might be, we have to control our first instinctual reaction. Take deep breaths and count, walk away, watch the clouds, take a run, do a yoga pose, sing—whatever it takes to detach or to separate yourself from your first reaction will work. Learning anything well and having success at something will give you confidence in your ability to just say no to your emotions and take control.

Once you can control your reaction, you are in a position to let your mind decide how to act by asking yourself what your long-term goals are and by making your choices accordingly. Is your long-term goal to make someone feel bad physically and emotionally, or is it to make yourself feel good physically and emotionally? Is getting in trouble in school your goal? Is watching someone in pain your goal? Or, is creating the kind of life you want for yourself and your loved ones what you ultimately want?

Ask yourself this question when you are tempted to seek revenge: What behavior would help me achieve my long-term goals, and what behavior would make it more difficult to achieve? That is the question that should dictate your actions, not saving face or showing off. Again, what are your goals, and what is the best way to obtain them?

THOUGHTS FOR TEACHERS

Curriculum and Pedagogical Suggestions: Literacy and Physical Education

How can school systems be serious about addressing character culture when they reduce recess or gym? How do you feel when you haven't had a chance to move around a bit during the day? Most people probably feel increasingly tense when they have to stay in one place for too long, and too often the slightest provocation can set them off. Everybody needs breaks to work smarter and better! Even though school systems are up against many financial and curriculum imperatives, it's still worth considering what an ideal educational environment would look like, if only because it gives you a goal to move toward.

To enhance both literacy and social skills, students need to learn how to identify and articulate their emotional states while also learning to gain control over them. Some parents and educators think these skills should be taught at home, but too often they're not. Because you are with your students for six or seven hours a day and because your success as an educator depends in large part on your students getting along with each other and feeling good about themselves, you must find ways to do it.

Gaining control over one's emotions has been one of the goals of human beings for centuries. It isn't easy for any of us to do this, especially for kids, with the news they see on TV and their relationships at home and school sometimes as poor role models. How can you accomplish this in spite of its difficulty? First, by modeling good behavior to your students. Kids learn from what they see. When you let a child get you going (and doesn't everybody?), not only are you in for a bad day, but you also broadcast the wrong message to your students. To yell, speak sarcastically or disrespectfully, or to cut off someone's conversation or questions casts doubt about how serious you are about maintaining a respectful and caring classroom. Nothing turns a kid off more than hypocrisy. Additionally, there is no better way of losing a student for the long term than turning your anger toward a kid.

Your behavior, while never perfect, must reflect your better angels as much as possible. You need to demonstrate how you can take a deep breath and not respond immediately to provocation but instead act with your ultimate goals in mind. If you slip, as indeed you will, you need to be willing to acknowledge your mistake and apologize to your students. To admit you are not perfect (and who is?) is a good way for your students to feel comfortable with their own failings and to help them trust your honesty and commitment to the behavior you are espousing.

How can you help your students become emotionally literate? For one thing, keep the communication flowing in your classroom. In the lower grades, morning circles are good. Find literature that is emotionally rich and intellectually provocative. It creates space and language for discussion about sensitive topics. This not only builds emotional and observational intelligence, an important element in their writing, but it is also the first step toward creating a culture of caring and consideration in your classroom.

The next step is to help your students gain some degree of control over their raging emotions. Teaching yoga, tai chi, karate, capoeira, or anything else that emphasizes mind control over the body should be a priority. How would school culture change if everyday day began with a few yoga exercises?

What sets kids off? Brushing up against someone they already have friction with, a teasing session that transgresses that illusive border between friendly and unfriendly, a rumor, competing for a boy or girl's attention. It goes on and on, and like in a dry forest, an errant campfire can be the spark for a blaze that will spread throughout your classroom.

Kids need to be aware of all these possible fight instigators and be able to catch them before the forest burns to the ground. To do this, begin a discussion about what kinds of slights, perceived or otherwise, could escalate. Role-playing these conflicts and their alternative resolutions is also good to do. Consider these ideas vaccines against the disease of classroom chaos.

Taming these fire-starters is also supported by learning to identify the physical feelings that emerge in your student's bodies when they feel threatened. Do their shoulders tense up? Do they breathe differently? Does their posture change? Helping your students pay attention to and identify these signs will let them know when they are about to lose control, and then hopefully they will be able to initiate behavior that helps them regain control. Remember, the mere act of noticing and identifying gives one a sense of control.

Make time for your students to discuss or write about times in their lives when they've let their emotions control them and consider whether the results were what they wanted. Ask your students if they have ever been able to thwart their self-righteous anger in favor of an understanding of the long-term consequences of their behavior. Can you set aside time for you and your students to discuss when you or they have lost the battle with their emotions?

We must help our students understand that controlling emotions is not unlike learning a sport or a musical instrument. Temporary failure is part of these efforts. One failure does not end the game. Hall of Fame baseball players are out two-thirds of the times they bat. Failure is opportunity, a chance to reflect, to discuss, and to try to make it right the next time.

Lastly, it is important that the entire school be on the same page, which is why your antiviolence work needs to be a whole-school initiative. If your community is aware of the potential for violence and has a collective commitment to avoiding it, there can be agreed-upon forms of intervention: moving someone away from a potentially violent confrontation or deescalating conflict through humor, just to name a few strategies.

Allow your students to talk about and decide what kind of behavior they would welcome and respond to when they feel their violence thermometer moving toward boil. Ask them to help you, as well, if they sense you are losing it in the face of the many challenges of being a teacher or an administrator. They will enjoy giving you advice, and it makes them feel you are committed to the same type of behavior you are advocating for them.

Chapter Five

Antonia, the Juggler

To Share or Not to Share?

Antonia didn't know what she wanted to do when she grew up, and as you can imagine, everybody gave her advice.

"Perhaps you should be a shoemaker? It is a nice profession. You can sit all day!" said Massimo, the horseshoer.

"Perhaps you should be a farmer? It is a nice profession because people are happy to see you—unlike my own profession," said Luigi, the tax collector.

"Perhaps you should become a carpenter? It is a nice profession. You make something that is lasting," said Salvatore, the fruit man.

Unlike all of her friends who, by the age of sixteen, had already chosen their professions, Antonia couldn't decide how she wanted to make a living. It was quite a problem. Her mother, father, uncles, aunts, brothers, sisters, and cousins all did their best to find a job that would fit Antonia's skills and interests.

"She certainly has a talent for speaking," said her father. "Perhaps law would be good?"

"She would make a good baker," said her mother.

"Yes, I agree," said her sister. "Antonia really likes to eat!"

"I think that Antonia would make a superb accountant. She has a head for figures."

"She is the sensitive sort," said her aunt. "She should be a poet."

"Perhaps she should make barrels," said another sister.

"Or a wheelwright," said her brother, "because her head goes around and around like a wheel!"

They all laughed, except for Antonia, who thought about it, thought about it, and thought about it but with no answer in sight.

One day, a brightly colored wagon pulled by a team of white horses came into the village. Outside the wagon, in gold, scripted letters, was the name of the woman who owned the wagon: Sabora. She drove to the center of the village, where the shops and their customers congregated. From the wagon came Sabora, with long, white hair and a long, black cape filled with stars, and from a colored cloth bag, she took three balls—and immediately began to juggle. Up in the air the balls went, under her arms, off her arms, behind her back. It wasn't long before all the townspeople stopped doing what they were doing and watched the impressive visitor.

They watched for almost an hour. It was certainly clear to all that they were watching someone who was a master at her art. When she finished, everyone applauded and threw money into a hat that she had set out for that purpose and went about their business, except for Antonia. She now knew what he wanted to do with her life. She wanted to become a juggler.

"Excuse me," she said shyly to the woman, who was now alone, gathering up her equipment to put back into the wagon. "Excuse me. Do you think you could teach me to juggle?"

Sabora looked up. "I am looking for someone to teach and you're the right age. I'll tell you what, I'll take you around and teach you to juggle, but you must promise to always remember that the most important lesson I have for you is that the joy of having a skill is to share it."

Antonia couldn't believe her good fortune. She jumped in the air.

"No problem! I'll remember."

She went back to her home and told her family that she would be traveling with and learning from the juggler. Worried at first about her leaving the village, they all felt Antonia's excitement and decided not to interfere. Her mother packed her some food, her father some clothes, and her brothers and sisters some books to keep her company. Then, her whole family and a large group of others from the village escorted Antonia to the village center to say goodbye. They waved as she got onto the wagon and set off for new lands and experiences.

Antonia and Sabora traveled from village to village. Antonia cooked and cleaned for Sabora, and in return, at each stop, Sabora taught her something new about juggling. First, one ball, then a second, and finally a third. It was difficult at first. One hand was weaker than the other, and the ball from that hand would always fly off and outward. With two balls, she rushed and rushed and pretended she was juggling, only to be slowed down by Sabora, who told her to take a pause between the two balls and left room for an eventual third ball. Three balls were very, very difficult, and she spent much of her spare time chasing them after they dropped and rolled on the ground.

But finally, she got it! Once she got it, she *really* got it. It wasn't long before Antonia was juggling the balls under her legs and behind her back.

Not only did Sabora teach Antonia how to juggle, but she also taught her how to make her living from entertaining others. She taught her where to set up in the town to gain maximum visibility (the village center); what to do if the police didn't want you to set up in a particular place (first, try to teach them to juggle and promise to put them into your act; if that doesn't work, ask them where a good place to set up would be); and how to get along with other traveling magicians, storytellers, and musicians (swap stories about the best places to travel where the people have the loosest pockets).

One day, Antonia was practicing her juggling. By now, she could juggle five balls and even fire clubs. Sabora watched, and when she finished, she said something that Antonia thought she would never hear when she began her apprenticeship under Sabora's tutelage: "Antonia, you've become a better juggle than I am. It's time for you to go out on your own to seek fame and fortune. I'll buy you a wagon, but you must always remember that the joy of having a skill is to share it."

Antonia went out with her own white horses and wagon, one with her name now scripted on the side in gold letters, and traveled first to the small towns and villages she and Sabora had traveled to. Later, her fame grew, and she traveled to small cities and then to larger cities. As her fame grew, she finally was asked to perform for the king and queen. Soon she was known as the best juggler in the kingdom, traveling to perform at the finest theaters, with red velvet on the walls and chandeliers overhead.

One day, as she traveled from one city to another, she came to her old village. Because she hadn't returned in many years and had some time, she decided to spend the night there to see family and friends. No sooner had she walked under the stone entry gates when she was surrounded by those who still recognized her.

"It's Antonia! Juggle for us!" a young boy yelled. "Juggle!"

She went into the village center and got out of her wagon, looking like a celebrity with a gold-sequined jacket, loose-fitting silver pants, and shoes that shined in the sun. She threw one ball, then a second, a third, a fourth, and a fifth. She juggled fire clubs and axes, pins and rings. There were more "ahs" and "ohs" than at a fireworks show!

As she juggled, however, she noticed a young lady about the same age she was when she asked Sabora to teach her to juggle. "Excuse me, Antonia. Would you teach me to juggle?" the young lady suddenly and unexpectedly asked.

She was very athletic looking, and Antonia could tell that, if she taught her to juggle, the girl would be able to learn well. As Antonia aged, her skills would diminish, and soon, the girl would become a better juggler than she, and then she would no longer would be known as the best juggler in the kingdom.

"No, I don't have the time," she told the young lady sharply.

But as she continued to juggle, Antonia noticed the young lady was watching her every move, and she began to worry that this young lady was trying to steal her tricks. So, for no reason clear to her audience, Antonia stopped juggling, gathered her equipment, and went into her old family home to think about what she might do to prevent this young lady from stealing her act and becoming a threat to her career.

Inside the house, Antonia juggled while thinking of what to do, until she worried that the young lady might be looking in through the window, so she closed the shutters. She worried that she might be looking into the cracks in the walls, so she decided to stop juggling all together. As she did, however, she began to feel weaker and weaker and weaker, until soon she could hardly walk, stand, or talk.

After a number of days, the villagers who hadn't seen Antonia since she had entered her home began to worry. A few worried villagers entered Antonia's home, and as they did, they were shocked at how sick and weak she looked. Soon all the villagers knew that Antonia was ill, and they brought in food and herbs. Nothing brought strength back to Antonia's limbs or spirit, until one day, the brightly colored wagon, pulled by the team of white horses, entered the village center. On the outside of the wagon was the name of the woman who owned the wagon: Sabora. Sabora got out of the wagon with her long, white hair flowing in the wind and her black cape filled with stars. No sooner did she throw one ball up in the air when she was told about Antonia.

She immediately stopped juggling and went to Antonia, who lay on her bed, now unable to move. The once vigorous young woman looked much older than her age, with her strength gone. Sabora shook her. "Antonia. Antonia. Antonia."

Antonia opened her eyes only slightly and looked up. "Oh, Sabora. What are you doing here?"

"The question is, What are you doing down there?" Sabora answered.

"A young lady is trying to steal my tricks, and if she does, I will no longer be the best juggler in the land."

Sabora shook her head. "You learned to juggle better than anyone I'd ever taught. You rose to unbelievable heights in your career, and yet, you forgot the most important lesson I had for you: that the joy in having a skill is to share it. Now get up and go out. Find the young lady, and teach her to juggle!"

"But," Antonia started, realizing how difficult it would be to carry out Sabora's instructions.

"No *buts*. Do it!"

With the strength she had left, Antonia raised herself from the bed; picked up three juggling balls; and, to the surprise of all the villagers, went out of her house for the first time in many, many months. Her eyes, unaccustomed to the sun, squinted.

"You!" She called to the young lady, who was crossing a street. "You wanted to learn how to juggle. Come here!"

Antonia took one ball and threw it to the young lady, then a second, and finally a third, and after a day of practice, as the sun's setting was giving the sky to the first stars of the evening, the young lady could juggle. She excitedly ran up to Antonia and said, "Thanks for teaching me to juggle, Antonia. I want to be a juggler like you. Would you take me around the way Sabora took you and teach me all you know about juggling?"

Antonia looked at her and smiled. "I'll take you around with me and teach you all I know, but you must promise to always remember that the joy of having a skill is to share it."

QUESTIONS FOR STUDENTS

- What do you think happened to Antonia in the story? Why didn't she remember or heed the advice given to her by Sabora?
- Do you believe that the joy in having a skill is to share it? Why or why not?
- Have you ever felt competitive toward someone? When?
- Have you ever done anything to make sure that the person you felt competitive toward didn't achieve what you thought they wanted to achieve? What did you do, and how did it feel? What were you afraid of?
- Has being competitive with someone ever hurt a friendship for you?
- Can we become successful in life without thwarting another's ability to achieve success?
- Do you remember a time when you shared a skill with someone? What was it, and how did it make you feel to do so?

THOUGHTS FOR STUDENTS

I remember hearing that people had secret recipes that they wouldn't share with others, and I wondered why. We've grown up with the idea that, if we have some sort of knowledge or skill that sets us apart from others, once another had it, we would no longer be unique.

Wanting to be unique, wanting to be better than, wanting to be the best at such and such certainly brings out some wonderful qualities in us. It makes us work hard and, if we are lucky, to be able to enjoy the results of our efforts. However, hoarding what we have can make us worried and nervous.

We worry that someone is going to discover something we feel is "ours" and nervous that once they do, we become less and not more. This feeling often comes from the idea that we are in constant competition with everyone around us, competing for prestige, for money, for girls or boys, for coolness, or for some sort of other perceived reward. It makes us feel always on edge and continually in protective and guarded mode.

When we feel that we are always on guard, it is difficult to ever relax and enjoy someone else's success because too often their success is viewed as our failure. We are often so worried that someone will overtake us that we not only avoid sharing our talents, skills, and knowledge with others but also sometimes go as far as sabotaging another person's success to make sure that they don't surpass us.

We do this by passing rumors around about the person we are in competition with, not sharing some information, passing along false information, or tripping him or her up in another way. I've had this happen to me. I was devastated. Luckily, we were able to recover our friendship. Of course, this also gets into how we apologize and forgive, which are topics for a later chapter. Here, I just want to point out how competition taken to its extreme might get you ahead professionally but will do so at the expense of those things that really matter: friendship.

I think one of the reasons we feel we have to compete with one another is that we don't learn in school how even very successful people have learned from others. Scientists don't make their discoveries in isolation. They read each others' studies. They work together with other scientists. They build on past discoveries.

Artists go to shows, look at books, even copy each other's work as they develop their own styles. Most artists live around other artists or at least hang out with other artists, so that they are easily able to speak with and help each other evolve their ideas in a setting of mutual learning. Baseball players share information about a certain pitcher's tendencies. Lawyers study precedent, how other cases have been argued and decided. Doctors learn from the successes and failures of others, in person and through studies. Mechanics learn the easiest way to remove a part from a car by watching others do the same.

Musicians go to clubs to hear and learn from others. In fact, many tunes contain riffs they've heard before and were influenced by. This is even more clear in today's world of digital music technology, where so much of today's music is put together by sampling. The social nature of music construction is now really indisputable. Knowledge is social, which means that, just as our language comes from everyone around us and before us, our skills, talents, smarts, and creativity all come from the same stew, with the continual introduction of new spices.

Think of how Antonia felt when she was hoarding her juggling skills and how her strength and power returned once she began to share them. We become bigger when we share and smaller when we don't.

I've certainly done both: withholding knowledge from others and competing with another when I thought their rise would lower my status. But, like Antonia, when I was able to rise above my fears and share, I felt better. It's like they say: a candle's light is never diminished when it shares its flame with another.

THOUGHTS FOR TEACHERS

Curriculum and Pedagogical Suggestions: Science and Inventions, Arts, Copyright Law

Our culture romanticizes individual genius that seemingly receives its inspiration from above. We venerate the one who captures our attention in our celebrity-obsessed culture. We believe there is nothing more important than having our fifteen minutes (or preferably more) of fame. Reality TV throws the winner-take-all mentality in our faces. Consequently, it is not surprising that we often resist sharing our expertise and skills.

How can we remind our students that, just as the great geniuses of the past needed a social context to work from, we need each other for success, as well? First, it is imperative to teach not only about the ones who "made it" but also about the ones who were part of the circle who helped that individual become famous. No idea, no great effort, no invention, vaccine, or academic or artistic breakthrough happens without an extraordinary effort on the part of many, many people. The more you teach about the social context of success, the more the true nature of creation is revealed and hopefully the less paranoid the next generation will be about sharing their knowledge and skills with others.

The issue of copyright is a fascinating place to start in this regard. Students could easily be drawn into debate and discussion about where the lines of intellectual property rights are drawn and transgressed. When are copyright restrictions so tight that they prevent creativity, and when do those who do the hard work not get rewarded because someone stole their creation? In rap music, for instance, sampling has been a big part of its creation, and many legal cases have been initiated about this and other artistic creations, where works of the past have been appropriated in service of a new creation. Who can borrow and who can't, and what are the justifications?

One place where these kinds of discussions are occurring is in the conversations about intellectual commons. The commons are what we collectively retain as part our cultural, ecological, and biological heritage. What is included and what is not included within this category, and how and when it is free to be used is of tremendous importance in many areas of contemporary society, from intellectual property rights to the control of seeds, plants, and even our genes. What a great way to link a science curriculum to our discussions about sharing.

In physical education, it is important to give credit to those who make things happen but might often not get noticed. In baseball, give credit to the player who successfully executes a sacrifice bunt or who hits a grounder to the opposite side of the infield to advance a runner. In football, call attention to the lineman who opened the hole for the running back or the defensive lineman who kept a guard busy while the linebacker came in to sack the quarterback. In basketball, help students notice how important the person who sets a good pick is to team success.

In music, learn about who influenced now-famous musicians as they developed their chops and fine-tuned their styles, how, for instance, Mick Jagger and Keith Richards of the Stones listened obsessively to the blues, Dylan to Woody Guthrie, and on and on. Everybody, professional or not, stands on a platform built by others.

Speaking of sharing, some young people simply haven't experienced the joy of sharing their knowledge, of teaching. It is important to give them opportunities to do so. Finding opportunities for your students to teach something they are good at would honor their own skills and help them feel like experts in the eyes of those they are teaching. It would also help them learn about the art of teaching and the stages of learning. It would introduce them to the joy of seeing someone they taught become, if not proficient, then better than they are.

Teaching about how innovation in any field is collectively generated and affording students the opportunity to teach and to learn from one another will go a long way in creating a collegial relationship in your classroom and in your school. Why? Because by doing so, it becomes clear that sharing knowledge doesn't diminish your own star but brightens everybody's. Or, as the old saying goes, thousands of candles can be lit from a single candle, and the life of the single candle will not be shortened.

Chapter Six

Alligator

All That? (Folktale from India)

Most people think that all alligators do is lie in the sun—and *rrrroooaaarrr*! But every once in a while, they walk around just to make sure the world is still there. Every once in a while they sharpen their teeth because everyone knows that the best part of an alligator is its smile.

But, nothing gets a boy alligator moving quicker than seeing a new girl alligator he'd never seen before.

One day, this particular alligator (you can call him anything you want because, as far as I know, alligators don't have names) sees a girl alligator he'd never seen before. She was quite beautiful. Her skin had lovely greenish-brown scales that reminded him of the most beautiful swamp mud he'd ever seen. Her bite had two lovely teeth sticking out from her mouth that looked like the tips of crab claws, and her eyes were like the stars the boy alligator saw in the night as he waded in the shallow waters of the swamp to pounce on some prey.

The boy alligator felt his heart beat like wood thrush wings, and he sharpened his teeth and went down to where the lovely alligator was lounging in the sun and said in a way that both shocked and surprised the girl alligator, "Yeah!"

The girl alligator looked at him, shook her head dismissively, and said, "Hrumph!" momentarily shocking and scaring that boy alligator away.

Not to be deterred, he went back to that girl, again lounging comfortably in the sun, and once again in his arrogantly confident way said, "Yeah!"

Well, that girl alligator looked at him, shook her head dismissively, and again answered, "Hrumph!" And, once again, the boy alligator, shocked at what he thought was such a rude dismissal of his charms, jumped away.

The third time that boy alligator tried to gain the lovely alligator's attention, he tried with the same flirtatious smile and growl, and the girl alligator looked at him more dismissively and with even more disgust than before. Then, making a mistake that many boys make, the boy alligator both did and said what he did and said before, except this time, he was loud enough to make the leaves of trees around the swamp sand. "Yeeaahh!"

As, as you can imagine—yup. "Hrumph!"

"I know," confidently thought the boy alligator. "I know what I need to do. I need to get that beautiful girl a present—something to eat!"

An alligator's favorite food is the heart of a monkey. They're sweet, soft, and very difficult to get because, as you know, monkeys are mostly in the trees and alligators are mostly on the ground. But, one day, a monkey jumped to the ground in search of a banana she had just dropped, and she saw that boy alligator.

"Oh, hey, alligator," she said with an innocence as true as the morning dew or a kitten with a ball of yarn.

That boy alligator couldn't believe his good fortune, and if you were there at that time, you would be able to see the wheels in his brain churning as he said, "Oh, hey, monkey. Say, monkey, I see that you are going to pick up a banana. Haven't you heard about the new fruit that grows on the island in the middle of the river? Twice as sweet as a banana and *three times* as big. Why don't you go get some?"

The monkey, with the banana in one of her hands and ready to put it into her mouth, looked at the alligator and said, "I'd love to, but I can't swim."

"Oh, that's too bad," said the alligator. "You know, I have some time. Why don't I take you over there?"

"You'd do that for me?"

"Yeahhhhh," Alligator said in his most charming way and with his most charming smile. So, the monkey jumped right onto the alligator's back, and the two slipped and slid their way into the water.

The monkey really enjoyed the water and was quite happy. She felt the breeze against her skin and said, "So nice of you, alligator, for taking me. So nice of you!"

The alligator looked at that monkey, and the only thing in his mind was how happy that girl alligator would be after he brought her that monkey's tasty heart. "Yeaaahh, I know," he said, with a charming smile that seemed to stretch to the nearest star.

The monkey watched the clouds float by above her, feeling happy with the world, until she felt herself get lower and lower in the water, first her feet, then her legs, and then her belly. Nervously, she said to the alligator, "Excuse me. Eh, excuse me, alligator. I'm sorry to bother you. I know that you are working hard to bring me over to the island where that wonderful fruit grows, but, uh, but, I feel that I am sinking."

The alligator smugly looked up at the monkey and with a knowing and mischievous look in his eyes simply said, "Yeaaahhh, I know."

Which of course shocked the monkey to no end.

The monkey continued to feel herself sink lower and lower into the river and, still believing that it was all some kind of mistake, said, "Um, I'm sorry, alligator, and I know that I'm being kind of annoying, but don't you remember that I told you that I couldn't swim?"

The alligator smugly looked up at the monkey and simply said, "Yeaaahhh, I know."

"Maybe you don't realize it, alligator," the monkey said, still believing that this story wasn't going to end the way it appeared to be heading, "but that means, if I go down into the river any further, I'm going to drown!"

By this time, the alligator couldn't help flashing a little self-congratulatory smile as he said, "Yeaaahhh, I know."

By now, fearing for her life and finally understanding that her death was exactly what the alligator wanted, the monkey couldn't help herself as she exclaimed, "And then I'll die!"

"Yeaaahhh, I know."

"What do you want me to die for?"

"I want your heart!" the alligator replied in the most confidently sinister way that the monkey had ever heard anyone speak.

But she was smart, this monkey. One time, the monkey was drinking some water at a lake, when a dragon came up from the bottom of that lake and, rearing its angry head, said, "If you put your lips to my lake, you will drown!"

But the monkey, not at all intimidated by that dragon, went to the side of the lake, took a long plant, blew out the insides of that plant, stuck it in the water, and drank—becoming the one who invented what we all know of today as the straw!

So the monkey, still slowly sinking into that river, started to laugh hysterically, just like her friend, the hyena.

"What do you have to laugh about?" asked the alligator, slightly offended because the monkey didn't seem impressed by his powers nor scared by her impending doom. "You're about to die!"

"I didn't think that you were soooo stupid," the monkey replied.

"What?" asked the alligator, with a mix of anger and confusion.

"You actually think that monkeys go out of their house with their hearts still in their bodies? No way! We could lose them out there. Before a monkey leaves its house, we open up our chest, take out our heart, and all the monkeys give their hearts to me for safekeeping. In fact, I put them in my special closet, where I still have one hundred monkey hearts, ones that the monkeys never came back for because they must have found ones they liked better while they were out in the forest."

The monkey noticed that the alligator was right with her, so she continued. "Yeah, I have a hundred monkey hearts in that closet, and I didn't know what to do with them until I met you, and then I remembered how much alligators like monkeys' hearts, and I thought that I wanted to pay you back for being so nice to me by giving you those one hundred monkey hearts."

Amazed at his luck, the alligator said, "You were going to give me one hundred monkey hearts?"

"I was, but I guess it's too late now, now that you are going to drown me."

The alligator thought for a second, wondering if he should believe the monkey. If he did and he was wrong, he might not get a heart at all. But, at best, he could get one hundred monkey hearts. He knew it was a gamble.

"Let's go back!" he said decisively.

So they did, slipping and sliding back to the land to the tree where the monkey said she lived. The alligator watched as the monkey scurried up the tree, while the alligator waited down below.

"I'm waiting! Throw them down!" he yelled.

But instead of throwing down one hundred monkey hearts, the monkey threw down a fur-covered nut, and it landed right on the alligator's head, splitting in two and pouring a milky liquid all over the alligator's face!

"Ow! That's no heart of a monkey!" he screamed.

"You're not as silly as you look," the monkey said. "See you later, alligator!" she laughed.

As the alligator went to the river with the milk pouring all over his face, you never guess whom he saw—the girl alligator! He was so embarrassed that he looked for a rock to hide under, but there were none big enough, and his tail kept sticking out.

But that girl alligator saw him and noticed the milky liquid pouring down his face. For the first time, she realized that he wasn't trying to be all that, the bomb, fresh, bad, or cool, and so, instead of making fun of him, she actually thought he looked kind of cute and said, in a more quiet and dignified way than he had, "Yeaaahhh!"

He, feeling the milk on his face and realizing how silly he must have looked, looked up at the girl alligator quizzically and said, "Huh?"

She looked at him again and said, "Yeaaahhh!"

He, still feeling confused, said, "Huh?"

She was getting more frustrated by his inability to understand that now, finally, without acting like he was all that he was kind of cute. She said again, "Yeaahhhhhhhh!"

He said once more, "Huh?"

"That's it," she thought. "I will leave no room for confusion!" So, she simply said to that boy alligator, "Come over here."

And you know what? He did! And from that time on, the boy alligator and the girl alligator waded and swam happily in the warmth of that river and swamp and in the joy of their love, every once in a while getting up to make sure the world was still there and every once in a while sharpening their teeth because everyone knows that the best part of an alligator is their smile!

QUESTIONS FOR STUDENTS

- Why did the girl alligator seem to like the boy alligator better when he had the milk all over his face?
- Have you ever liked someone better when you could see something that was not perfect about him or her? Tell us the story.
- Have you ever seen a boy shouting out what he thought was a compliment to a girl on the street? What was the girl's reaction?
- Boys, do you think that girls enjoy having their privacy interfered with in that way?
- Boys, have you ever tried to show off to impress a girl? When and what did you do? What was the girl's reaction?
- Girls, have any boys ever tried to show off or act "all that"? If so, how and what did you think?
- Why do you think that boys have to often show off or act all that to impress a girl or to get her to notice him?
- Do you think that the way the boy alligator tried to attract the girl alligator's attention was a respectful way to meet? When someone uses the kind of tone that he did, what is the message that you think they are sending? What might be a better way to meet someone you think is cute and interesting?
- Have you ever seen boys whistling or calling out to girls in the street or from cars? How do you think that makes the girls feel?

THOUGHTS FOR STUDENTS

Boy and girl stuff has always been and always will be with us. Figuring out how to be a boy and how to be a girl is part of who we are, one of our jobs, you might say. How it actually happens, how we know how to behave as a boy or as a girl, is a complicated process that is a combination of how we feel inside and how we think we should feel. Sometimes the way we think we should behave locks us into a straitjacket, not only affecting how we move, how we behave, what we wear, what we like, and how we speak, but also how we feel about ourselves and how we treat each other.

In this story, the boy alligator thought that he had to be all that to impress and interest the girl alligator. He acted in the way he had probably seen other boys act by interfering with and disrespecting the private space of a girl alligator. Boys, you can usually walk down the street without being bothered too much, except occasionally by a rival group of boys or an older boy wanting to prove himself at the expense of younger boys, but imagine if you had to deal all the time with loud whistles, catcalls, strange and scary sounds, and even being touched. It would restrict your freedom and would cut back the places and the times you felt that your neighborhood or city was yours to enjoy.

That is what girls and women experience every day. The boy alligator, obviously a stand-in for boys in general, knowingly or unknowingly added to the girl's sense that her freedom to move about was restricted and that the outside world was not safe. Again, boys, imagine that the roles were reversed. You would probably feel threatened and uncomfortable, wouldn't you, by someone behaving toward you in the way that the boy alligator behaved toward the girl alligator? How terrible not to be able to feel at home and relaxed in the place where you walk!

In some ways, though, the boy alligator's behavior wasn't really thought out. Again, it probably was what he had seen others do or what he had seen on TV or in the movies if, of course, he could ever really watch a film! In films, TV, and videos, boys often seem to have a right to speak with girls like the boy alligator spoke with the girl alligator.

In this story's case and probably in most cases, the boy's behavior didn't get the girl but, in fact, angered her. She had little or no respect for him and treated him like some kind of pest or child. The learned behavior didn't get what the boy alligator wanted. Often this is the case with learned behavior. We do it because we've seen others do it, but it really doesn't give us what we want.

It's not easy to be a boy at any age. You think that you are expected to be a warrior, tough, independent, without confusion, and a fan of sports and wars and not necessarily of flowers, birds, and painting. What if you liked all of these? What if you only liked to dance? What if you would rather sit around and watch the clouds than clobber an opposing lineman in a football game? Well, the idea that there is only one way to be a boy can be quite restrictive. Why can't boys be both, a football player and an artist? Sometimes the *should* gets in the way of what is real.

Boys also feel like they have to be independent, deal with things on their own, and not share anything they are thinking about or worrying about because to do so admits vulnerability, and that is a sign of a boy's weakness and a signal that they are just not tough enough to go it alone. There is certainly strength that comes from making others not feel bad because you are going through tough things and courage needed to deal with what comes at you unexpectedly in a dignified way, but this cowboy or soldier mentality can also make you feel quite alone.

Generations of American soldiers never talked about what they experienced during battle, and it left them holding the burden of their grief and confusion all alone. Imagine carrying all that all by yourself and never letting your friends and family into what you were dealing with or going through? There are a lot of lonely moments and a lot of moods unexplained.

What if we gave ourselves permission to just relax and to be who we are without worrying about how we think other people want us to behave? What if we could choose our friends, our activities, our behavior, and our clothes based on our personal preferences rather than on what we think are the expectations of others? What if we gave each other the permission to be who we felt like being in all of its weirdness, unpredictability, and seeming contradictions? It would be a lot more comfortable for everyone with a lot less pressure, a lot less unspoken anger and confusion, and a lot less violence, as well.

When the boy alligator finally stopped pretending how cool he was (because it was very difficult to pretend to be cool with coconut milk dripping down your face), the girl alligator started to pay attention to him. It was when he actually showed a little insecurity that the girl alligator thought he might be all right to speak with and to get to know.

I can't promise that walking around with milk on your face or a hole in your pants or by dropping your lunch tray on your way to your table will soften the heart of anyone you like, but I can say that you might feel better about yourself if you allow others to see, just a little, how human you are.

Like everyone else, you are composed of a little confidence, a little confusion, a little cool, a little independence, a little nerdy, and a little needy. Will you get the person of your dreams? I'm not sure because everybody has their own expectations about who they want to and will talk with, but I can tell you that by being as real as you can, you will inspire others to do the same and help to create a community and an environment that will make it a bit easier on all of us to become someone we really like.

THOUGHTS FOR TEACHERS

Curriculum and Pedagogical Suggestions: Gender Studies, Media Studies, and Social Studies

It is important to help widen the range of possibilities for what it means to be and behave like a boy or girl. Many problems emerge when students, or anyone for that matter, try to adhere to gender role expectations. For boys, especially those close to and in middle school, these role expectations become even more problematic as puberty kicks in and the importance of fitting in often trumps being yourself. This can create dissonance and confusion that easily can turn into violence as a subconscious way to resolve internal tensions.

In this story, the braggadocio of boys and the expectation that a boy has to be all that to attract a girl produced one confused boy alligator. Without any ability to speak like a real person to someone from the other sex, the boy alligator was left with only his showing off or his presentational personality to attract the girl alligator's attention, leading him to annoyingly and antagonistically take over the girl alligator's space with his leering "Yeaaahhh!"

When boys drive down the street or stand with each other on the street corner and whistle or make comments to a girl passing by, they often don't realize that this is a form of violence. They think it is OK and expected and that girls will like this kind of flattery.

Very few boys spend any time imagining what would it be like if the situation was reversed, with a group of girls were whistling at them while they walked down the street. Even more jarring and a probably a more accurate example would be for a heterosexual boy to be walking down the street and a group of much larger gay guys standing on the corner started to hit on him, although this is much less likely to happen.

The gaze is all-powerful and important. From the security of a stable place (with a group of guys secure on a street corner or inside a car with the windows open), you have the power in a street meeting. The girl is walking, and the boy is secure in his place, often fortified by his friends. The whistle or catcalls leave the girl feeling vulnerable to his power and not sure about how far the harassment could go.

Boys need to realize how this behavior restricts a girl's freedom to use the street like anyone else. Take Back the Night is a good place to start to introduce boys and girls to this issue (https://takebackthenight.org). It is a foundation that sponsors events to "end sexual assault, domestic violence, dating violence, sexual abuse and all other forms of sexual violence." It highlights the importance of girls, young ladies, and women being able to walk the street, day or night, without the threat of harassment or worse.

Rigid gender expectations hurt young men, as well. Boys need to understand that the stereotype of the cool dude, the one who has it all together and doesn't need to talk about anything, is an antiquated and limiting vision of masculinity. Not only is this idea no longer very attractive to girls, but also it is harmful for boys and men.

Soldiers coming home from war often understand very well how trying to maintain their military identities of perfectibility and impenetrability becomes a straitjacket. Believing that their experiences are theirs alone to deal with, many returning soldiers are unable to cope with civilian life, often blowing up unexpectedly in anger, acting in other unusual and scary ways, or being so full of horrible and unshared memories that their relationships often suffer and break down. Bringing to school an ex-soldier who has endured the psychological straitjacket imposed by maleness upon coming home from war would be a good way to start this type of discussion.

Creating an opportunity for boys to share their thoughts and feelings helps to break down the myth that men don't have issues they are concerned with. I was asked to work with a group of about fifty sixth-grade boys who were having some difficulty in school. They were bored in school, and many were getting in trouble, starting fights, and disrupting class, among other things. I asked them what in life they were interested in. They answered girls, their friends, and music. I asked them to bring in rap that talked about these subjects, and for the next few weeks, they did. Music was a good springboard into a sensitive conversation. Things calmed down.

Another time, I was working in a high school session with a group of about twenty boys dealing with street and gang violence. I asked them how their walk changed from inside to outside their homes. Inside, they acted like you can imagine anyone acting inside the privacy and security of home: hanging out walking loosely and doing silly things preparing to leave, but the moment they walked outside, the walk was more purposeful, eyes hardened, backs straightened—they went "street."

Once you notice that public identity and its presentation are malleable, once you recognize that you are not locked in, you are then able to consider the cost of your choices and whether they are interfering with or supporting your short- and long-term goals.

Behavior is often adopted at an early age and often as a means to defend oneself against needs unmet or even pain delivered. On a simple level, if we don't get much attention as children or if that attention is negative, one of our defensive postures is to back up, psychologically speaking, to hide ourselves from the outside world. This might work when the world around us is inattentive or hostile. The danger is, however, not unlike in the act of the great mime Marcel Marceau, where the clown's eternally present smile can't come off once the show's over, it is difficult to remove the armor when one's life situation finally allows for safe intimacy.

Many unaware young and older men are trapped inside an identity that might have been useful at one time yet, as they got older and their circumstances change, is no longer beneficial. The more you can help your boys understand how their behavior is learned and consciously and subconsciously supported and maintained, they will have an easier time realizing that the key to unlocking the no-longer-useful self is theirs. Once freed from the restrictions of vestigial behavior, it opens up room for sensitivity, empathy, and vulnerability to emerge.

Creating this kind of trust in your classroom is very important and valuable. Becoming aware of how we trap ourselves inside our defensive behaviors and our culturally received identities is a good place to start boys and girls on the journey of gaining control over who they are and how they behave.

Here are some ideas for making this ongoing struggle visible:

- Have your students compile a list of gender identities they notice in the media: TV, video games, advertisements, and so on. Ask them to look at which ones they aspire to and why. Is that really who they are, or is it something they feel the need to construct in order to be cool and socially successful? How do advertisers benefit by suggesting certain identities for us to select? Ask your students to consider the cost of buying into one of those behaviors. What toll can it take on their bodies, their friendships, their wallets, and their own personal freedoms?

  This bit of media awareness is a good wake-up call for understanding how the world of corporations benefit from the identities they are offering. Ask your students if and how much they want to be influenced by those whose interest is in making money from them rather than really supporting their search for a comfortable and sustainable way to be themselves.

- Create a curriculum and a culture in school that prioritizes the practice and conversation about music, theater, storytelling, and visual art; it is a good way to keep violence at bay. You can't get kids to understand how violence hurts them until they are able to unlock those sides of themselves that they deny are even affected. The arts, at its best, asks questions, challenges assumptions, and is often concerned with issues that require and foreground sensitivity and self-awareness.

- Introduce boys to role models, both in the media and in real life, who are not John Wayne or Rambo types but instead are boys or men whose heroism is expressed through sensitivity, vulnerability, the ability to understand and overcome their fears, and the courage to pursue their destinies and follow through with their principles.

  Point out that heroism does not always depend on an encounter with violence but can be expressed through honesty, commitment, and the struggle through whatever makes you uncomfortable. The study of alternative heroes can be part of both English and social studies classes. Looking at mythology, of course, and the inimitable work of Joseph Campbell for the essence of the heroic is essential to introduce your students to a new model of the hero.

- Listen to music that introduces discussions of gender issues. This can easily be part of the music or English curriculum.

- Study returning veterans. This can be connected with social studies.

- Look at women's safety issues, including harassment. This should be part of any health and social studies curriculum.

Chapter Seven

Nasrudin

*The Wise Fool and the Meaning of Clothes
(Folktale from Turkey)*

*Nasrudin is the wise fool, a folkloric character who was born in Hortu
Village, in what we now call Turkey. His fame spread throughout an area
that we now call the Mideast or the Levantine. What is a wise fool? Well, it's
someone who doesn't appear to be smart because his behavior is a little out
of the ordinary. He seems to think differently from those around him, and this
enables him to understand the world with more insight than those who think
and act conventionally. The following is a Nasrudin, or Hodja, as he is
sometimes called, folktale.*

Nasrudin loved working in his garden, a garden he made beautiful in spite of
how dry and dusty his village was. The fruit from his trees were like pieces
of edible jewelry; his vegetables were lush, like the dew in the morning, and
dripping with flavor. His flowers were so bright with color that they gave
light to evening's darkness. Nasrudin's garden was the envy of all the villagers, who came to learn from and marvel at his knowledge of which fruits,
vegetables, and flowers to plant so that each would feel protected and grow
like children in a loving home. In fact, he inspired others in this dry village to
work equally hard, until soon his village was known throughout the region
for its fruits, vegetables, and flowers.

One day, Nasrudin, dusty from clearing rocks from the area around his
home where he hoped a new garden would bloom, was surprised by his
friend Ömer.

"Peace be with you, Nasrudin."

"Peace be with you, Ömer," replied Nasrudin, unable to look up from the dusty earth as he single-mindedly continued to work.

"Nasrudin, I am here to remind you that tonight is the night of Hamid's big party, so make sure you stop your work in time to wash up and put on clean clothes so that you will get to the party by sunset."

"Thank you, Ömer."

"See you later."

For a moment after his friend left, Nasrudin was excited about going to the party. After all, Hamid was the richest man in the village, and although Nasrudin had never been to his house, he had heard much about it: about the rugs with delicate patterns of colorful silk, about the furniture with inlaid precious stones, and about the grand room with gold and silver paintings on its ceiling. Almost more importantly, he heard that the food that would be served was so wonderful that each bite would take you to heaven. He was excited to go, but as was usually the case, Nasrudin lost track of time while he was working in the garden. Before he knew it, the sun began to set, giving a golden glow to the desert mountains beyond the village.

"Oh no!" shouted Nasrudin. "I forgot about the party! I didn't go home to clean and change! What am I going to do?"

It took a few minutes before Nasrudin calmed down and said to himself, "Why do I need to go home and change my clothes anyway? These are my people. I am known and respected by all. I will go to the party looking just the way I am!"

Nasrudin put his tools away and walked to Hamid's house. Dusty as the desert itself, Nasrudin walked through the door of the house that made him feel as small as a crumb of bread on a table. He looked up at the ceiling and was stopped in his tracks by its beautiful drawings. The floor was as glorious as he had imagined, and the carpets looked like his well-crafted and -maintained garden. He was so hypnotized by what he saw that, at first, he didn't realize he was surrounded by the villagers, friends he had known from childhood. Once he noticed, he was happy to see each one.

"Hello, Fatma. Hello, Ömer. Hello, Layla. Hello, Cemal."

But as happy as Nasrudin was to see everyone, he was ignored. It was almost like—no it *was* like he was invisible! Almost as troubling, he was invisible to those who were passing through the guests with plates of food, which called out loudly to his empty stomach. Each time Nasrudin reached for a tray filled with food, it was pulled away, leaving him off balance, almost falling to the ground.

A bell was rung, and all of the guests were ushered into the dining room. The guests, chatting with each other like birds in the spring, rushed past Nasrudin without a word and to their seats at the many tables filling the elegant dining hall. By the time Nasrudin arrived into the grand hall—"No seats for me!"

He thought for a while and said, again to himself, "Because I can't sit down and eat with everyone anyway, I have time to go home, wash, put on new clothes, and come back to the party before everyone has finished. At least I will have some dessert."

Once home, he washed and put on new clothes. He left and retraced his path, now under the star-filled night, and walked back into Hamid's house and into the party, where just a little while ago he had been ignored. As he walked in, he realized that there must have been a delay in serving. All the guests were still talking to one another, their plates unused. No sooner did he walk in than Nasrudin was spotted by all of his friends who, one by one, happily shouted out "Nasrudin, sit here with us!"

"Nasrudin, there is a seat here! We've been waiting for you!"

"Nasrudin, tell us about the garden!"

"Nasrudin!"

"Nasrudin!"

"Nasrudin!" One by one, they called out for Nasrudin's company until Hamid, the owner of the house and the host of the party, noticed the clamor and said, "Nasrudin, I see that you have finally arrived. Please, do me the honor of sitting next to me at the head of the table."

Nasrudin liked that, and with a wide smile on his face, one as large as a crescent moon, he made his way past the guests.

"Hello, Nasrudin," one by one they all said, and he walked to the honored position in the center of the table at the head of the room.

Hamid put his arm around Nasrudin, looked at the guests, and said, "It is my great honor to have Nasrudin at my table. He is a man whose work in his garden has inspired us all and without whom our village would be just another bit of sand in the endless desert. But through his work, Nasrudin has made his garden and the gardens of others come alive, and our village now shines like a candle in the night. As I see now that our food is finally before us, may we say a toast to this wonderful person, Nasrudin. May your good health be twofold."

With that, all the guests in the dining hall sat, ready to eat. But, in this village, it was traditional to wait until the honored guest puts the first bit of food into his mouth, and that night, the honor would go to Nasrudin. With all eyes facing him, Nasrudin put his bread into the baba ganoush, the mixed eggplant, but instead of putting it into his mouth, he put it into his baggy trousers. An audible gasp filled the shocked room. Nasrudin then put his bread into the hummus, the mashed fava beans, and instead of putting it into his mouth, he put it into his shirt, and the guests sat in stunned disbelief. Then finally with his bread, he picked up the dolma pilaf, and instead of putting it into his mouth, he put it into his cloak. All focused on Nasrudin, who was disgracing the host of the party, the richest man in the village, by putting his food into his clothes. Hamid couldn't believe his eyes.

"Nasrudin, I put you at the head of the table, at the place of honor, and we are all giving you the honor of being the first to eat, but you disrespect us all by putting your food inside your clothes rather than in your mouth. How could you disgrace my guests and me in my own house?"

Nasrudin looked up from his plate, a sly smile on his face. He then looked at Hamid and began to speak. "Hamid, I wish you no ill will. Your hospitality tonight was beyond reproach. However, when I first came here tonight and had on my clothes, still dusty from digging, I could get not even a hello and certainly no food. I was a ghost to all—invisible. I go home, clean, and put on new clothes, and suddenly I am like a god, desired by all. This made me a bit confused until I was finally able to figure out why those who ignored me now celebrated my arrival. I realized that you must have invited my clothes here and not me, so I thought it only fair to feed my clothes first before I had a chance to eat."

QUESTIONS FOR STUDENTS

- Why do you think the villagers ignored Nasrudin when he first walked into Hamid's house?
- Have you and your friends ever judged, made fun of, or gossiped about someone because of what they wore? When and how and about what?
- Do you agree with the proverb "Clothes make the man," or do you agree with "You can't judge a book by its cover"? Why?
- Did you ever worry about what to wear, finally decide what to wear, and then thought you made the wrong choice and were embarrassed by what you chose? When?
- Are there different looks in your school that you can pick out from the clothes that someone is wearing? If so, can you name them and the clothes that are indicators? Have you ever been surprised by someone who you thought was one way because of their clothes and they turned out different from what you expected? Tell us about that time.
- Has there ever been a time when you felt judged by something you wore and you resented it and felt more than the sum of your clothes? When?

THOUGHTS FOR STUDENTS

For many, clothes are often strong indicators of whom they will like, be friends with, and will include in their groups. However, I have found that outward appearances don't tell the whole story about someone. In fact, when you think someone is one way because of his or her clothes, you are often surprised and quickly understand that truth is more complicated. It is probably a good idea to hold your judgment about someone until you get to know him or her rather than jump to a conclusion based on what they are wearing.

Of course, that's not to say that you are not immediately going to assume something about a new person because of their clothes; we all do. It only means that you shouldn't take that initial judgment seriously. Just notice that judgment and let it go as you are getting to know that person. After all, you wouldn't want someone to judge you by what you chose to wear one day to school or how your hair looked at a party or for the sneakers you played on the court with.

One's clothes can isolate a person from a group of kids or become material for teasing. You know how it goes: Someone chooses a shirt that's too bright or a pair of pants that don't quite have the right fit, and the others make fun of that person, either behind their back or directly to their face. We all make clothing faux pas or mistakes or just wear clothes that appeal to us but not to others. How about letting up on each other a bit to make it easier for all of us to make a mistake every once in a while. Hey, we're all human, right?

Lastly, there are many people who simply don't have the money to buy clothes that you think might be cool. Of course, everybody has a different idea of what is cool. Some people can't afford something fashionable. Some people's families are tight on money, and their money has to be put toward rent, food, fuel, and maybe medicine first. It's not your schoolmate's fault that they don't have the same ability you might have to buy stylish clothes, so why give them a hard time because they don't?

This kind of thing often happens with sneakers, where the right brands can run into big bucks. Why put that pressure on others and, in fact, on yourself to buy things you can't afford? Why tease them because their family's finances or economic priorities don't support purchasing all new and expensive clothes? The more we can let others be with clothing choices, the more comfortable we will be with our own choices and necessities. While it is true that certain clothes are necessary to wear to a job interview or work or to enter into some clubs or restaurants, you and your friends in school do not need to make a big deal about it. Clothes are what you wear, not who you are.

THOUGHTS FOR TEACHERS

Curriculum and Pedagogical Suggestions: Fashion and Media Studies

How many of you remember being really uncomfortable about what you were going to wear to school or to a party? How many remember wanting to buy a piece of clothing that you thought was just right and your parents told you they couldn't afford it? How many of you were teased because of something you wore? No doubt most of you remember how important certain clothes were for helping you feel part of a group and how mortified you were when you couldn't wear what you lusted after.

Try some media awareness work with your students to help them unpack how advertising influences their sense of self, their ordering of the rest of the world, and the visual language and goals for their aspirations.

We all live inside a consumer republic. That is no secret. Even after 9/11, George W. Bush, the president of the United States, told us to go out and shop. A large part of the United States' economy depends on how the world spends their money on consumer objects, be it clothes, cars, houses, appliances, and so on. If an entire culture is built around consumption, it's a good guess that a large amount of money will be used to convince people that it is important to buy certain items. It seems that all the reasons given for purchasing can be boiled down to this: We are not complete until we have this or that.

We are inundated with images of the perfect house, the perfect body, the perfect family, and the perfect car, and all we need to do to become perfect is to purchase perfection in whatever way we are convinced to do so. If only *you* could buy the necklace, *you* will look like that model in the photo. If only *you* could buy that new house with the three-car garage, *you* will be considered a success in life. If only *you* could buy that car, that suit, that dress, then *you* will be what *you* always aspired to be, or at least whatever it was that *you* wanted to appear like.

Here is where consumerism gets kind of funny. The line between how you want to project yourself and who you are inside is often blurred. Often people mistake what they want to project with what would make them truly content, and even more problematically, they often forget that there is even a difference. They try to, piece by piece, put together a series of presentational components (the house, car, sneakers, bling) that will supposedly allow them entry into a group they aspire to be part of. They don't consider that this fix will not really bring a sustainable sense of well-being. As the old folktale tells us, "we mistake the reflection of the moon on the lake for the real one."

It is important to help your students realize that advertising gives someone else's blueprint for self-creation by seducing them to purchasing the fool's gold of identity. This discussion would be valuable for young people who are busily trying to fit in and fear that they won't. Analyzing advertising in all of its forms, from billboards to Internet ads, will take the power away from these messages. By studying advertising and its goals, as well as the subtle and often-hidden ways it works, we take its supposed neutrality away. This will help our students to be on the lookout for how advertising is manipulating all of us as a prelude to picking our pockets.

Clothes do not make the man or woman unless we let it. A new barbecue, car, or summer home are not the Mason–Dixon Line for your success or failure, nor should they determine whom you like, ostracize, or tease. Media awareness is a good curriculum choice as you attempt to create an environment where everyone feels comfortable about being who they are. A classroom or a school intelligently armed against our corporate and advertising tsunami of images is the best defense against a school culture where its members are judged on their ability to adhere to someone else's image of what is cool and what is not. This is also fine-tuning our critical thinking skills at its best!

Chapter Eight

Two Woodchucks and the Art of Forgiving

There were two woodchucks—let's call them Bollywood and Snickers. They were friends, best friends. They did everything together: helping each other dig deep holes under the earth, warning one another when they noticed a trap being set, sharing news about an unprotected garden, and sharing the news that a house with particularly tasty flowers was now being guarded by a fierce dog.

No one, not even other woodchucks in the neighborhood, thought that it was possible that woodchucks could cooperate as well as those two did. Everybody knows that woodchucks do what they do all by themselves and jealously guard and defend their territory, but these woodchucks, to the amazement of all, worked together and helped one another with everything, from foraging to relaxation.

From the time the woodchucks emerged from their long winter's nap to the time they happily saw each other on that first day in the late spring, when the grasses and flowers were set before them like a king's banquet, until it was time to sleep through another winter, the two were together. From the moment they woke up in their tree-filled neighborhood in a small town near a large pond in southern Rhode Island, Bollywood and Snickers would meet and search for a nice garden to breakfast together.

All kinds of things, predictable and unpredictable, were part of their days together. On one day, they'd try a new flower, whose petals were as sweet as candy. Another day, a garden where they had feasted for many years would suddenly have a fence around it, and the two would find the perfect spot to dig under it—laughing as they did!

Sometimes, the two friends would notice something very sad. As they strolled through their neighborhood, they would see another woodchuck, one

75

they recognized, caught inside a trap, probably attracted to the beautiful broccoli or the rinds of a watermelon that the two-leggeds had put in there. In a little while, the two would watch a two-legged pick up the trap and put it into the back of their rolling vehicle. As the two looked, they knew it would be the last time they would see that woodchuck. Exactly where the two-leggeds took that woodchuck was not known. It was the place far away, the place from where no one returned, and the place no woodchuck wanted to go.

Bollywood and Snickers would look at one another and say, "We will never, ever let the other be taken away to the land from where no one returns! Never!"

The two woodchucks had a good time together: eating, digging, running quickly away when the two-legged creatures came out of their houses with severe faces as the two woodchucks were munching on some new shoots in the garden. As one would eat, the other would stand up straight and watch for the two-leggeds because sometimes those creatures angrily threw rocks and sometimes they even had a long, long stick that exploded loudly.

"I'll watch your back, and then you watch mine," they said to each other, and both laughed. It was kind of a joke the two had between them because, in fact, both knew that neither watched each other's back.

One day, when Bollywood was taking a nap in the hot noonday sun, Snickers, who was too hungry to sleep, walked around the neighborhood in search of a midday meal. In a garden newly planted, he noticed some green shoots coming from the earth. The small stalks tasted good as he nibbled at them, oblivious to everything around. Noticing some pieces of watermelon and cantaloupe, he moved to eat them, as well. Suddenly, he heard the thick metallic sound of a door crashing behind him. When he looked up, he realized that he had been trapped. Behind him was the shadow of a two-legged with one of those large exploding sticks in his hand—a gun!

"OK," said the two-legged. "I got you now. No woodchuck is ever going to again eat the vegetables I worked so hard to plant!"

Snickers shook and shook and shook. He didn't know what to do. He tried to dig his way out of the trap but couldn't. He tried to look mean and ferocious, but that didn't work either. He nervously thought about the land of no return, where he was sure to be taken. Would it be a dry land with no plants? A land with giant dogs? A land where the ground was so hard he couldn't dig a hole for his house? Each thought made him more and more fearful until an idea calmed him down.

"Mr. Two Legs, Mr. Two Legs." (Don't ask me how he learned to speak English.)

"Yes," said the two-legged.

"Mr. Two Legs, you got the wrong person here. I was sent here by my boss, a much bigger and hungrier creature than I am. He's in charge of the entire neighborhood. He gets all the other woodchucks to bring him vegetables and fruits because we are all scared of him. Without him, none of us would attack your vegetables. We would be quite content with the grasses and plants that grow wild in our neighborhood. But, the boss tells us that we have to bring him the sweetest shoots from your new plants and the colorful flower petals that taste like candy!"

The two-legged put down his exploding stick. "You don't say," he said. "Then where is this boss?"

"I can take you there if you let me out of this trap."

"OK, I will, and then I will follow you, but if you try to run away, I will shoot you in the back."

Snickers finally knew what "watching your back" meant. "OK, I won't run away. I promise."

The two-legged released Snickers, who felt good no longer being confined inside the trap. He led the two-legged through the neighborhood until he came to Bollywood's home, where his friend was still sleeping in the coolness of the underground tunnel.

"OK, here it is. The boss lives in here."

"What is the boss's favorite food?"

"What?" asked Snickers.

"You heard me. What is the boss's favorite food? I want to trap him."

"Um, Um, Um."

The two-legged creature pointed his exploding stick toward Snicker's head.

"Celery. He loves celery."

As soon as those words came out of his mouth, the two-legged threw a burlap bag over the poor woodchuck's head and tied the bag up at the top.

"OK," said the two-legged. "If I don't catch your boss in a few days, I will drop you into the pond."

Snickers was carried back to the two-legged's house and left in the yard. He heard the two-legged pick up the trap and leave. After that, all was quiet except for the birds and a wind that rustled softly through the trees.

When Bollywood woke from his nap and came out from the hole, he noticed to his happiness and surprise a few nice long and fresh stalks of celery looking at him like an old friend.

"Hmmm," he thought. "How lucky am I. This wasn't there when I went to sleep. I'll eat some and then tell Snickers to come get some."

But as Bollywood walked toward the celery stalks, he heard the metallic door slam shut, and he knew he was trapped. He tried to escape, first by digging a hole, then by bouncing again and again against the sides of the trap, and finally by screaming for help. A few hours later, hungry and thirsty, he heard and smelled a two-legged. The two-legged picked up the trap. Bollywood snarled and bared his teeth, making loud and scary sounds that his mother had taught him to make, but the two-legged was unafraid. Tipping from side to side as he was carried, Bollywood tried to stabilize himself. Soon the tipping and swaying stopped. Bollywood was in the back of the two-legged's car.

The engine was loud, and for the first time, Bollywood was taken from his neighborhood and was moving faster than his four legs had ever taken him. A while later, the car stopped and its engine was shut off. Bollywood knew from the smells that this was somewhere he had never been. The two-legged opened the door, got out, opened the back of the car, and picked up the trap. Bollywood swayed back and forth. By now, having had no food or water for quite a while, the trapped woodchuck was so weak he could no longer snarl or growl. He knew that he had been taken to: the land of no return!

The two-legged put the trap down and opened the door. The two-legged bent down. Bollywood didn't know why, so he curled up fearfully into a corner. The two-legged opened the door and tapped on the back of the cage. Bollywood hung onto the metal bars. The two-legged then picked up the trap and tipped it over, and still, Bollywood clung on. Finally, the two-legged banged the walls of the cage with a stick, and it frightened Bollywood so much that he released his hands from the trap, and out he went. He was now free, and Bollywood ran and ran and ran until he understood that the two-legged could no longer harm him.

But, now where to go? Bollywood explored the forest in the land of no return. Although there were no houses with gardens, there was plenty to eat and drink, and it wasn't long before the strength that had left his body returned. There were flowers that pushed up from the mud, small ferns shaped like question marks that were tasty, and plenty of water. But, there were none of the fresh garden flowers or the tasty vegetables from his old neighborhood and, worst of all, no Snickers!

Bollywood missed his best friend more than food and water, and after feasting for the first few hungry days on the food in the forest, nothing seemed to taste good anymore. He was lonely, and as he moped around, he realized that he had to make it back from the land of no return!

But, how would he do that? No one, as far as he knew, had ever made it back from this land. No one! But Bollywood was determined to see his friend Snickers once again, and after eating and eating and eating and drinking and drinking and drinking, Bollywood started his journey home. Bollywood's sense of smell and sight guided him. A familiar smell this way, not a familiar one that way. He dodged the two-leggeds' rolling monsters. He avoided their traps. He ran quickly past their dogs and silently made his way around a pack of wild coyotes. He made wrong turns that led him astray. He came to rivers rushing so fast he couldn't make it through them and was swept away, only to emerge soaking wet far away from the path he was following. And with all that, with all of those trials and tribulations, his one thought was getting home and back to his best friend.

Finally, after the longest journey Bollywood had ever taken, one that left him exhausted, he was there! Everything looked and smelled familiar. There was his hole, a bit clogged up with rocks and dirt, but he recognized it immediately. He was back! He would clean up his home and find Snickers.

Down into his tunnel he went, removing the dirt that had fallen in during his time away. He felt the familiar wet earth and smelled its coziness. There were even some new, pretty blue flowers, whose smell and taste put a smile on his face.

"Hey, Bollywood. Hey, Bollywood."

Bollywood looked up from his meal, and there was Ollie, the opossum, whose long, skinny tail Snickers and he would always laugh at.

"Hi, Ollie."

"You're back, I see. Back from the land of no return."

"Happily so."

"Say, you must be really angry at Snickers. What are you going to do?"

"Angry?" asked Bollywood.

"What? You didn't know?"

"Know what?"

"I was right there when it all happened. You mean you didn't know that Snickers, to save himself, took the two-legged to your house, and the two-legged left the trap there with your favorite food, celery?"

"What? He wouldn't do that. He's my best friend."

"Yes, he did. Hey, Zorro," Ollie called over to a raccoon that Bollywood knew, as well.

"Hey, Bollywood. Welcome back from the land of no return. I guess they have to change that name," Zorro laughed. He always did at his own jokes.

"Hey, Zorro. Tell Bollywood. Tell him how he was trapped. Tell him."

"Sure, sure. Yeah, I saw it. Snickers was in the trap, and the two-legged had an exploding stick in his hand when he came to fetch it. Snickers was shaking something bad. So then, Snickers says that it wasn't his fault that he was poaching the two-legged's food and that it was the fault of someone he called the boss and said that he'd help the two-legged get the boss if he let him free. So, he led him over here while you are napping, and he left the trap with your favorite food, and the next thing we all know is that you are gone!"

Bollywood couldn't believe his ears. His best friend? The friend he had wanted to see more than anyone? The friend whose friendship pushed him to be the first ever to return from the land of no return? Bollywood refused to believe it.

"It's true."

Bollywood looked up. It was Baltimore, the oriole, pausing from eating some grape jam left for him by the two-legged. "I saw it all. It's true."

Bollywood knew that he had to find Snickers. Snickers would tell him what happened. Those others were just jealous of their friendship. They always were.

Bollywood walked over to where Snickers usually feasted at this time of day, and there he was, nibbling on the little white flowers that grew up between the times that the two-legged cut the grass. In spite of all he had heard about what Snickers had done, he couldn't but help feel his heart leap and his face break into a smile as he saw his best friend.

Snickers looked up, and he couldn't believe what he saw—Bollywood!

"Bollywood, you're back!"

Snickers ran over to Bollywood, and the two had little tears in their eyes.

"Bollywood, where were you?"

"I was taken by the two-legged to the land of no return."

"How did you get back?"

"It was a long and difficult journey. I will tell you the story sometime, but first, I have heard something I must share with you. I can't believe it, and I don't want to believe it. Ollie, Baltimore, and Zorro told me that you led the two-legged to my house to save yourself. That's not true, is it?"

Snickers thought for a second, just long enough to convince Bollywood that it was true.

"No, I wouldn't do that to you," said Snickers. Bollywood heard the words he wanted to hear, but he could tell from the way they were said that they were not true.

Bollywood walked away, his head facing the ground as he did.

"Hey, Bollywood, where are you going? Let's go get something to eat. Let's roll around in some cool dirt. Let's go make the neighbor's dog bark. Come on, Bollywood. Let's watch each other's backs. It's so great to have you back! Get it, have you *back*?"

But Bollywood just walked away.

After that, the two gathered food, napped to get away from the sun, escaped from dogs, avoided traps, ran fast across streets so the two-leggeds' rolling machines wouldn't squash them. All seemed normal, but it wasn't because the thing that made Bollywood's and Snickers's life so much fun was no longer. Their friendship was gone. Oh, they'd pass each other walking around the neighborhood. They'd nod to each other as they did. But nothing was left of who the two used to be.

The summer passed, and Bollywood and Snickers got fat from their summer feast. As the clouds grew darker and the air colder, as the birds flew south and the leaves turned color, both knew, as did all the woodchucks all over the land, that it was time for the long sleep. Bollywood and Snickers worked to make sure their underground homes were safe and secure for the long nap. Both knew that the time of feasting was over until they woke up and were greeted in the spring by the fresh green sprouts once again.

On a day when the fall's chill was in the air and when the smell of the leaves was particularly strong, Snickers came over to Bollywood's home. He had tears in his eyes.

"What's the matter, Snickers?"

Snicker's sniffled back his tears. "I have a confession to make before we go on our long sleep. I did bring the two-legged to you, and I did tell him about your favorite food, and I have been so miserable since then. I was so scared of being sent to the land of no return that I didn't know what to do. I am so, so sorry. Can you forgive me? I want us to be friends like before. Life is not worth living without friends like you. Please, Bollywood, forgive me!"

Bollywood looked at his once–best friend, and he felt tears in his eyes. He, too, missed the friendship, and he, too, knew that life was not as rich as it had been when the two were inseparable. A strong, cold wind blew through the trees and shook the two. The sky, now thick with gray, dropped its first small snowflakes onto their faces and onto the ground. They both looked up at the bare trees above them. They watched the squirrels with nuts in their cheeks scurry to hide them for the long, hungry winter. The last geese were in traveling formation and were leaving to warmer spots on this large planet. The time had come.

Bollywood looked at his friend and, with tears in his eyes, said, "I miss you too. I understand how you were so scared and how it made you act. But, as for forgiveness and whether we can again be friends, I will let the long sleep tell me what to do."

Snickers and Bollywood went down into their tunnels, and after a very short time, they again were asleep.

QUESTIONS FOR STUDENTS

- Do you think that Bollywood should forgive Snickers? Why or why not?
- Do you think that Bollywood *will* forgive Snickers? Why or why not?
- Do you think that, even if Bollywood forgives Snickers, they will be able to be friends again? Why or why not?
- Have you ever had a friend who did something bad to you? If so, what was it, and how did you handle it?
- Could Snickers have handled his apology better? If so, how?
- If you had been Bollywood, how would you have reacted after Snickers apologized?
- Is there a right and a wrong way to apologize? If so, what do you think should be part of an apology?
- Does the person who was wronged have a responsibility to accept another's apology? If so, why? If not, why not?

THOUGHTS FOR STUDENTS

Forgiving someone is very, very difficult. When you feel that someone has done something to you, it's difficult to trust him or her again. Yet, we all have done something to somebody we are not proud of and have hurt someone we cared for.

For instance, how many of you had a really good friend who, like all of us, had some quirky or uncool parts? Maybe they had a laugh that sounded like a horse neighing. Maybe they had a habit of eating a stinky sandwich every day at school for lunch. Maybe they were really into some singer who everyone thought was lame. When you got to middle school, you wanted to be accepted and were worried that your friendship with this uncool person would make everyone think that you're some kind of a geek, as well. So, you decided to drop your long-term friend.

When your friend wanted to get together, you would say you had something else to do. When they sat down with you at lunch, you suddenly moved to be with someone from the cool crowd. Maybe you even did something worse, like joined in when your new friends were teasing your old friend for their stinky sandwiches or odd laugh.

You lost this old friend, and you had a new group of friends to hang with. Suddenly and unexpectedly something happened in your life that made you sad: your parents split up, your grandfather died, a girl or boy you liked started to hang out with someone else, whatever. You realized that the only person you trusted to share that information with, the only person you really wanted to be with, was that person you dissed. So, you found them, and they wanted no part of you. You were smart enough to realize why, so you apologized and said that you wanted to be friends again. They wanted no part of you because they thought that you were only using them. You apologized again and again: "I'm sorry for what I did. Please trust me!"

But they couldn't.

Trust is very hard to repair once it is broken. When you have a friend and you share important time with them, you create a bond that you don't share with everyone. You reveal your uncool parts, and you trust that they won't leave you. It takes time to build trust with another person and time to repair it when it is damaged—if, that is, you ever can.

So, the first thing to remember is to not break the trust in the first place. How? First, through honesty, being honest with your friend. That's what trust and friendship is based on. Almost everything between friends is OK if you can be straightforward. There are times when you want to explore new friendships but don't share that with your old friend. We don't say, "Hey, I want to hang out with so and so today. I'll see you tomorrow, though." We don't communicate and often just leave the other person, your old friend, hanging.

Of course, there are times when you grow apart from someone, when you realize that your friendship is over. That happens, but the break doesn't have to be total. You still can speak with that person, occasionally touch base with them, and certainly you don't have to tease them to make your cool currency more valuable. Good friends are good communicators. If a problem comes between two people, they can speak about it and, most importantly, take some responsibility for what went down.

This is partly what a good apology is about. Apologizing is not just about saying "I'm sorry," although it is a start. It is also about letting the other person tell you how angry they are and how you hurt them. It's about taking responsibility and letting your friend know who you were at the time when you did something jerky. For instance, in this example, you can say, "I acted like a jerk toward you because I was afraid that I wouldn't be accepted as part of this group. I'm sorry I felt the need to separate from you, to join them in teasing you, and to not include you in this new group of friends."

OK, that's part of it, but then you have to repair the damage. "OK, I know that you don't trust me. I know that I was a dope and that you can't trust me now. Let's just start slowly and do some things together."

In the story you just read, it is not just that Snickers left the friendship with Bollywood; in the process, he also did something really, really bad to him. He betrayed him. He set him up to be exiled to the land of no return so that he wouldn't have to go there himself. This kind of thing happens. Friends do betray one another because the other person makes them insecure, because they want what the other person has, because they are threatened by the other person, and so on.

It is a terrible thing, and it has happened to me. In my case, as in Bollywood's case, this friend apologized (after many years, in my case), and like with Bollywood, I didn't at first know whether to accept the apology. But, I realized after talking to my friend, hearing his apologies, and realizing my resentment toward him and my unwillingness to accept his apology, I was putting more rocks in my mental backpack. Accepting an apology, a meaningful apology, clears the air and helps you to get rid of your anger. You don't necessarily have to renew your friendship to the level it once was, but by simply opening up again, you release yourself from the burden of resentment and anger.

I know that you might say, "That's not realistic. How can you forgive someone who did something bad to you?" True enough, but there are many examples when a person or a group of people did far worse to others than what my friend did to me or, believe me, what friends of yours did to you. For instance, in South Africa, there was a time when the white government set up something called apartheid, which grouped people into racial groups (black, white, colored, and Indian). Residential areas were segregated, sometimes by means of forcing people to move from their homes.

The government segregated education, medical care, beaches, and other public services and provided black people with services inferior to those of white people. A lot of violence was needed to enforce these laws. After much protest, both within and outside South Africa, the apartheid laws were removed, and blacks and coloreds, who were by far in the majority, were able to control the government. Many worried that those who had suffered so greatly from the violence legalized by apartheid would seek revenge.

To make sure this didn't happen, those who had been called "black" and "colored" and who now controlled the government set up a Truth and Reconciliation Commission, where victims of terrible abuses because of apartheid were invited tell their stories to the entire country. Those who committed these terrible acts of violence could also give testimony and request forgiveness and freedom from imprisonment.

Horrible things were heard, horrible abuses of people based on nothing more than the color of their skin. While there were certain failures, the Truth and Reconciliation Commission was a success, and revenge, by and large, was not part of South Africa's new nation-building process.

This was one example where people were able to admit the terrible things they did; to beg forgiveness; and, for the most part, received it. Amazing yet true! We all have the ability to own up to our bad sides and to forgive someone else's bad behavior. In some, larger way, forgiving someone is like applying a small patch to a much-patched bicycle wheel. It lets the wheels keep turning, even as we notice its many former holes. We are all human, after all. Perhaps you can remember that when someone says to you, "I'm sorry. Please forgive me."

THOUGHTS FOR TEACHERS

Curriculum and Pedagogical Suggestions: History, Global Studies, and Religious Studies

If you can help your students with this one, you should all get rewards!

Forgiveness is an extremely difficult act and a topic that has taken up many pages in the books of many religions. It has engaged the minds of great philosophers, as well as everyday folk like us, and has lots and lots of listings in a simple Google search. Why? Because forgiveness is an act we've all had had to contemplate, both as someone who sought forgiveness and someone from whom forgiveness was requested. It, along with its counterpart, vengeance, form much of the basis for our legal and moral systems, as well.

Some say forgiveness is healthy for those practicing it, relieving us from physical and psychological stress and letting us shed the psychological baggage of blame and recrimination. Others say that forgiveness can, if not used correctly, be a way of denying one's anger and self-respect and a way to allow injustice to continue unchallenged.

The day of Yom Kippur in the Jewish calendar is devoted to seeking forgiveness. Confession is an every-Sunday way to do the same for Catholics. There are hundreds of books about how and why to forgive. There is a Forgiveness Alliance and a Champion of Forgiveness award given by the Forgiveness Alliance. There is a nine-step forgiveness program written by Stanford University's Dr. Fred Luskin. Take a look at it:

1. Know exactly how you feel about what happened, and be able to articulate what about the situation is not OK. Then, tell a trusted couple people about your experience.
2. Make a commitment to yourself to do what you have to do to feel better. Forgiveness is for you and not for anyone else.
3. Forgiveness does not necessarily mean reconciliation with the person who hurt you or condoning their action. What you are after is peace. Forgiveness can be defined as the peace and understanding that come from blaming what has hurt you less, taking the life experience less personally, and changing your grievance story.
4. Get the right perspective on what is happening. Recognize that your primary distress is coming from the hurt feelings, thoughts, and physical upset you are suffering now, not what offended you or hurt you two minutes—or ten years—ago. Forgiveness helps to heal those hurt feelings.
5. At the moment you feel upset, practice a simple stress management technique to soothe your body's flight-or-fight response.
6. Give up expecting things from other people or your life that they do not choose to give you. Recognize the unenforceable rules you have for your health or how you or other people must behave. Remind yourself that you can hope for health, love, peace, and prosperity and work hard to get them.
7. Put your energy into looking for another way to get your positive goals met than through the experience that has hurt you. Instead of mentally replaying your hurt, seek out new ways to get what you want.
8. Remember that a life well-lived is your best revenge. Instead of focusing on your wounded feelings and thereby giving the person who caused you pain power over you, learn to look for the love, beauty, and kindness around you. Forgiveness is about personal power.
9. Amend your grievance story to remind you of the heroic choice to forgive.

There must be so much literature and conversation about forgiveness because everyone has to deal with it. If you can help your students learn to ask for and receive forgiveness, it will reduce the potential for violence inside and outside your classroom.

There are a number of ways that forgiveness study can segue into your curriculum. The first step, though, is to let students know that they are not alone in dealing with the issue. Second, help them realize that small moments of apology and forgiveness happen every day. It helps hone their observational skills to notice how many times an apology works to create social harmony in the inevitable small incidents of everyday life. For instance, someone bumps into someone on the subway or at the market and says, "Sorry." Usually this simple act of apology allows the other person to ignore being pushed or bumped and to say something like, "It's OK. No worries."

This mutual recognition of the potential for misunderstanding and retribution allows both parties to move on without any repercussions for an unintended incident. Things can get much more complicated when the simple act of seeking forgiveness doesn't get articulated, especially if the two people know one another and, worse still, if they hold a grudge toward each other. An unintended push, shove, or stealing of one's seat in school, for instance, can be interpreted as purposeful and can provoke an act of violent retaliation. Have your students ever experienced something like that? Can they write a story about it?

Now, it would be nice if forgiveness can always be asked for with a simple "Sorry" and received as swiftly with an equally simple "No problem." When the perceived or real act is not an everyday mistake but appears to be a more deliberate and calculated act, a simple "Sorry" won't cut it. Students need to learn how to ask for forgiveness if indeed they have done the act they are accused of doing, be it shoving, stealing, or cutting in on someone's boy- or girlfriend.

It is almost impossible to forgive someone unless the other person deeply and sincerely apologizes. The apology needs both to come from an understanding of the pain it caused and to include an honest look at why offender did what they did.

The offending person needs to exhibit both contrition and vulnerability. The power relationship between the two people needs to change for forgiveness to be granted. When one is acted on in a negative way, it temporarily gives power to the one who did the deed. When the perpetrator admits that they were acting from an array of motives that they were unable to control, asking for understanding shifts the power. Additionally, the person to whom the act of psychological betrayal or violence was directed needs to have the space to tell the other how they felt and how it affected their life. They need to be heard, so to speak.

It is also understandable for the injured party to ask for some form of recompense. This does not mean money, unless of course someone stole money from another. Recompense means that the perpetrator needs to understand their responsibility to repair any damage they caused—through damaging someone's reputation, sabotaging someone's efforts, and so on. Only after all these criteria are met can the perpetrator reasonably expect forgiveness. The power balance between the two needs to be equalized and the damage healed.

However, you can't force someone to forgive. People like to hold grudges. It gives them a sense of their own self-righteousness and often a reason to blame others for their perceived problems. It is also, as we all know, very difficult to remake a friendship with someone you no longer trust. How can we help our students forgive without having the expectation that the friendship will be completely repaired and reconstituted?

Again, back to enlightened self-interest, or deep selfishness. By asking students to reflect on how it feels to carry around anger day after day, we begin to create an awareness that holding a grudge doesn't hurt someone else as much as it hurts you. Carrying anger in one's mind and body is taking up room from other, more positive feelings. It is also creating a site of misdirection by incorrectly blaming any disappointment or anger you feel in general on the person whom you still haven't forgiven. This doesn't allow you to search for the real reasons you're angry or disappointed in life.

The connection between the personal and the global in the area of forgiveness studies is no more evident than with the South African Truth and Reconciliation Commission. To this day, people around the world are amazed at how black and colored South Africans were able to forge reconciliation rather than revenge. All is certainly not perfect in South Africa, but think of what could have happened if the majority, to whom such pain had been afflicted, used their newly won power to institute a regime of revenge. How were those whose lives so negatively affected able to find a way to collectively forgive, heal, and move forward?

Studying Truth and Reconciliation Commission is a great way to link your social studies and forgiveness studies. Where did the idea for a commission come from? How did it work? What kinds of crimes were articulated? How did the population react to the exposure of those crimes? How was forgiveness sought? How was it granted?

Unfortunately, there are many other examples where injustice toward minorities or between one country and another were and are still are large, important parts of our political and social landscape. Genocides, colonialism, institutionalized discrimination, and slavery have all been, unfortunately, part of our global history.

However you feel about these examples of brutality, it is difficult to deny that injustice was perpetrated. How did those other countries attempt to heal wounds created by those behaviors? How did they ignore them? America, for instance, still has not come to terms with either its history of slavery and segregation or its violent theft of lands previously owned by its native populations. How has the ignoring of all of these issues affected history and contemporary life? Does ignoring or denying them bring about a repeating cycle of violence rather than collective healing and reconciliation?

These are fascinating and important questions for your students, and their study could go a long way toward helping to make their own issues with forgiveness more visible, accessible, and hopefully easier to resolve. Will Bollywood be able to forgive Snickers after he wakes up from his hibernation? Will the world's populations be able to apologize and forgive for past injustices? Tune in tomorrow for another episode of *As the World Turns*.

Chapter Nine

How the Grouse Earned Their Name

There was once a large flock of big, fat birds that lived in a meadow filled with wild flowers and apple trees. Each morning in the fall, the birds would gather in groups of friends under the apple trees and feast on worms drawn to the apples fallen from the trees. When stuffed and happy, the birds would lie down in the meadow under the sun without a care in the world. It was a bird's paradise.

One day, a hunter looking for food for his village passed through the meadow and noticed those big, fat birds feasting on the worms. Being a man of patience and intelligence, he decided to come back the next day and the day after that and the day after that until he was confident he knew the everyday habits of those big, fat birds. Being a man who thought before he acted, he understood that, if he used his gun to kill the birds, he would only be able to take one bird each day back to his village. He understood that, upon hearing the gun's explosion, the other birds would flee.

After a week or so of watching, thinking, and planning, the hunter came back with a large net. As a group of birds feasted, he dropped the net onto their heads. Those birds, in a panic, ran this way and that, this way and that, running into the net, and were, of course, unable to escape. Soon tired from all this work, those big, fat birds lay down to sleep, making it quite easy for the hunter to surround them with the net, tie them up, and put them on the back of his horse. He brought them to his village, where a big pot of boiling water was waiting for those birds!

Every few days, once the last group of big, fat birds had been eaten and digested, the hunter came back and put his net over another group of birds and gathered them up, and soon, they, too, were put into the pot of boiling water and eventually eaten. Again and again, more and more birds were taken and eaten. The other birds in the meadow were so busy feasting that they didn't notice their numbers were dwindling. When finally they did notice, the remaining birds came together and imagined all sorts of theories about what had become of the others.

"It just must have been their time to join our cousins in the sky."

"No, I think they were swallowed up by the earth and turned into food for the trees."

"The giant worms must have punished them for eating the smaller worms."

It seemed that each of the big, fat birds had a theory, and because none of the birds wanted to stop eating long enough to watch what was actually happening, no one saw what happened to the others in their flock. One day, though, after still more big, fat birds disappeared, one group of birds, who were the smartest of those big, fat birds, decided to take a day off from eating to try to figure out just why the other birds in their flock were disappearing. None of the theories they heard seemed correct. They had seen no birds in the sky flying toward the sun and noticed no hole in the earth, and surely, no worms were large enough to eat a big, fat bird.

It wasn't long before they saw the hunter, his horse, and the net. The hunter put the net over a group of birds, who were so busy eating and eating and eating that they didn't even bother to notice. By the time they realized that they were covered by the net, it was, of course, too late. The big, fat birds ran this way and that to escape. Instead of escaping, they ran into the net. Soon, they were so tired that, like the other birds, they were easy pickings for the hunter, who wrapped his net around them and put them on the horse. Soon they had gone to their very, very hot death!

Those very smart *and* very fat birds, now that they had seen how their cousins had been captured, decided to teach the hunter a lesson. They talked and talked and talked, trying to decide what to do. I'm not sure who said it first because, as is usually the case, one idea leads to another and then to another and then to another until no one really knows where the good idea comes from.

But here's what was decided: This group of very smart *and* very fat birds would eat the worms as usual. Then, as the hunter's net was dropped on their heads, in a "one, two, three," they would spread their wings, and in another "one, two, three," they would fly into the air, taking the net with them. In a final "one, two, three," they would fly out from under the net, leaving it to fall empty to the earth. They were all excited about this idea. They were sure it would work and complimented each other on their idea.

"You are so smart!"

"Without you, we never would have come up with this idea."

"Me? It was your idea."

"Mine? Nah."

"Wait! We are all pretty smart to come up with such a smart plan."

"You're right; we are one smart group of big, fat birds!"

They all laughed and shook and laughed and shook until they all fell down and laughed and shook some more.

The next day, this same group went out into the meadow under their favorite tree. They ate and they ate but with one eye looking out for the hunter. After a nice, long feast, the birds noticed the hunter approaching. They smiled at each other in conspiratorial anticipation as they continued to eat. The hunter came closer, and the birds kept eating, until the hunter threw the net over the birds. The hunter couldn't believe how easy it was to catch these very fat and, he thought, very stupid birds. One of those birds called out, "One, two, three!" The big, fat birds spread their wings.

"One, two, three!" The big, fat birds flew up in the air, supporting the net with their wings.

"One, two, three!" The big, fat birds flew out from under the net, and the net dropped empty to the ground. The big, fat birds laughed and laughed as the hunter stood there without a single big, fat bird to take back to his village!

You never have ever seen a group of happier birds in your life than those big, fat birds who had just fooled the hunter. Those big, fat birds couldn't even speak because they were laughing and shaking so hard. Finally, catching their breath, they were able to speak.

"How smart we are!"

"How well we all worked together."

"I couldn't do it without you."

"Nor I without you!"

"We are one smart group of birds!"

They continued to laugh and laugh and laugh, rolling in the grass, down the hills and into the trees.

The next day, the hunter came back and that same group of big, fat birds did the same thing they did the day before.

"One, two, three." They spread their wings.

"One, two, three." They lifted the net.

"One, two, three." They flew out from under the net, and the net fell empty onto the ground!

The birds laughed and laughed and laughed, shook and shook and shook, and rolled and rolled and rolled and told each other the nicest things as the hunter stood empty-handed.

"You're the best!"

"No, you're the best!"

"You're the smartest."

"You're the strongest."

"No, you're the strongest."

Day after day, day after day, day after day.

"One, two, three." They spread their wings.

"One, two, three." They lifted the net.

"One, two, three." They flew out from under the net, and the net fell empty onto the ground!

One day after those big, fat, and very smart birds had once again fooled the hunter, they gathered as usual in the meadow to laugh, shake, and roll, when one of the big, fat birds said, "Boy, I am sooooooo happy that I thought of that idea to trick the hunter!"

"You?" said another. "But, that was *my* idea."

"How could that have been your idea? You've never even had a thought," said a third bird.

"Without my strength, we never could have even picked up that net," said a fourth bird.

"You, strong?" said another bird. "Your wing couldn't hold one of my feathers!"

"I had to work extra hard just to make up for how weak you are!"

So those big, fat birds, who had indeed outsmarted that hunter, began to argue.

"I am the strongest."

"I am the smartest."

"Without me, we'd be inside some villager's body!"

"Oh yeah?"

"Oh yeah!"

The next day, when those big, fat birds again were underneath a tree to feast on worms, their fight continued.

"I am the strongest."

"Without me, you'd all be gone."

"None of you would have come up with this idea if it wasn't for me!"

"Hey, get your wing off my wing!"

"Your beak is touching mine."

"Your legs are too long."

Suddenly and seemingly without notice, the hunter came and dropped the net onto those big, fat birds, but this time, instead of the "one, two, three," those birds just kept fighting.

"If you are so strong, pick it up yourself."

"If you think you are so smart, you come up with a new way to get out of this net."

"Hey, get your beak off my wing!"

"Your wing is in my face."

And so on and so on, until the hunter tied up the net and took those big, fat, and still quarreling birds away, put them on his horse, traveled back to his small village, where upon arrival he dumped them all into the pot of boiling water. Wouldn't you know it, though, those big, fat birds continued to quarrel, argue, and complain, even as the water was getting warmer and warmer and even while they were being cooked!

"I was the one who thought of the idea."

"I am the strongest."

"Get your beak away from my wing!"

"It's your fault that we are in boiling water."

"My fault? My fault? It was you who refused to lift your wings."

The villagers watched and listened to those big, fat birds quarrel and argue even as they boiled. As you can imagine, it was quite a sight. The villagers had a word for those who fought, complained, and quarreled. The word was *grouse*. You know, "Stop grousing, and get ready for school!" So, from that time on, those big, fat birds had a name. You probably can guess what that word is. From that time on, those big, fat birds were called grouse. Look it up, and you'll see. I kid you not. The dictionary might not tell you the story of how that name came to those birds, but I just did, and now you know.

QUESTIONS FOR STUDENTS

- Have you ever ruined a friendship because you and your friend started to compete against one another? If so, when, and how do you feel about it now?
- Have you ever worked together with a group of people for something you all cared about? When you did, how did it feel?
- When you started working with a group toward a common goal, were there some people you didn't like? Did that feeling about those you didn't care for change as you worked together? If so, how?
- Do you work better when you are competing or when you are working together with a group? Why?
- Have you ever been in a situation similar to the one in the story, where a group with whom you worked well began to argue with each other and, once you all did, you lost your power? Describe the situation.
- Have you ever accomplished something with a group of people that you feel you couldn't have accomplished on your own? What and when?
- If you had been one of the birds in the smart group and you saw the fighting break out, could you have said or done something to stop it? What?

THOUGHTS FOR STUDENTS

I love working together as a team, where each member has a role and each person's contribution is honored and no individual takes total credit for success nor is blamed for failure. So much more can be accomplished when individual energies are combined than when individuals are at odds with one another. When we are competing against each other rather than working for a common purpose, we all lose. We plot, and we scheme. Unfortunately, this kind of behavior is all around us. Just look at reality TV, *Survivor*, for instance, where everyone is made to feel that they cannot trust anyone else.

What a way to live, huh? Some would say that competition is the natural order of things, meaning that we as a species are hardwired for competition—you know, "eat them before they eat you" kind of philosophy or, as philosopher Thomas Hobbes called that view of the world, "the war of all against all." I'm not ruling out that there is a partial truth to this way of understanding the world. I'm not saying that there are people who are motivated by cutthroat competition. I certainly once was much more so than I am today, but I have also realized its cost.

I remember when my best friend in sixth grade said that he wanted to be president of our class and that I should be vice president. "No way," I thought to myself. "I want to be president, and he can be vice president." All of a sudden, even though I never said anything to him, I began to view our friendship differently. I realized that we were in competition. It changed the nature of our friendship, from one of best buddies to good friends who were wary of each other. I forgot who even became president, but I do remember that I felt less close to my friend after competition was injected into our friendship. Was it worth it? Probably not.

We surely live in a world where there is competition, but we don't learn enough about the other side of our nature: about how we are naturally cooperative, as well. We learn about great geniuses, but we often don't learn about the team of people who helped those geniuses create great ideas. We all study people like Jonas Salk, the inventor of the polio vaccine, but how many of us know about the scientists who built the foundation on which Jonas Salk built his ideas?

We learn about great artists like Picasso and imagine that somehow his genius came out of nowhere, metaphorically speaking that he dropped from the sky one day with an idea about how to paint many perspectives onto a two-dimensional canvas. We rarely hear about his circle of other artists or the museums and studios he visited. The same with great musicians, philosophers, inventors, and others.

We learn about the tip of the iceberg, the genius, but we don't learn about who else was there to help the genius work out his or her ideas. In sports, it's the same: We celebrate RBIs but less so who got on base or advanced the runner. We celebrate running backs who gain a lot of yards but celebrate those linemen who cleared the way or the wide receivers who created distractions for the defense a lot less.

I'm not saying that those others never get celebrated. Of course, they do. All I'm trying to point out is that often the individual is celebrated and studied more than the team of people who helped make it possible for the individual to succeed. In our celebrity-obsessed world, where individuals rather than groups of people are celebrated, we often feel that either we are the one who is noticed or we are the one who remains invisible. Celebrity and fame are seen as scarce commodities and ones that need to be fought for.

The birds in this story were at first saved through cooperation. The origin of their idea about how not to be caught was unclear. Great ideas are really like that. They grow from the ideas of others, discussions, books, articles, and environments conducive to innovation. This knowledge is widely accepted in many domains but now especially in the tech sector, where the social nature of innovation is widely understood, and tech companies' campuses are created to facilitate ease of social contact.

When one bird in the story began to brag about his idea, it made the other birds, once satisfied to celebrate everyone's role in creating the successful idea, worry that their contribution to this strategy would be ignored. Once paranoia set in, no one was content to celebrate the social origins of their idea but, instead, felt they needed to gain individual attention, while minimizing everyone else's contribution. The same thing happened when one bird tried to get credit for their superior strength. The cohesion of the group suffered, and it became less four wheels moving together in the same direction than a collection of four wheels fighting to go in whichever direction they pleased. You saw the results.

I'm not saying that some competition isn't OK. I just want you to understand what you are giving up when you are constantly in competition with one another and advancing yourself at the expense of the group. I also want you to notice how pleasurable it is to work in a group to achieve a common end and to recognize that everyone's contribution toward that goal is essential to your success.

The other day, I filled up my car with gas. As I was pulling out, I saw two big, tough-looking, leather-jacket-wearing motorcyclists trying to put a large hog, as they call it, up a ramp and onto a truck. Now these guys were probably not people whom I would have had a lot to do with—not that I wouldn't like them—but we wouldn't have found ourselves around each other very much. Our interests, I'm guessing, were probably very different.

So, these guys are struggling and arguing and having difficulty with the weight of the cycle. I got out of my car and offered my help. We got the bike onto the truck. They thanked me. I smiled and went about my business. I realized a couple things: One, I enjoyed helping; two, I enjoyed the fact that they hadn't expected help from someone like me, who probably looked more like an old university professor than someone whose strength could help them; and three, I realized that none of us or even two of us could have done what we all did together. All three of us were needed to successfully accomplish the task.

We need each other to complete tasks of all kinds. We are smarter working together than alone. We learn new things by building on the knowledge of others. Let's not let competition get in the way of that truth!

THOUGHTS FOR TEACHERS

Curriculum and Pedagogical Suggestions: History, Science, Physical Education, and Business

It is difficult to ask your students to cooperate with each other when schools stress competition over cooperation and if your content minimizes the importance of social context while foregrounding the individual's role in history.

Back in the early 1960s, a seventh-grade math teacher, after every quiz he gave, would line up his students in the back of the room in the order of their scores, last to first. Those who always finished in the middle were mortified about the possibility of falling behind those who finished higher, who in turn were scared of finishing in any position less than near the top, and those at the bottom lost interest in math altogether. How about the one who finished first? It was no guarantee of contentment and comfort. There would always be another competition.

That's the way it is when people are being measured and sorted solely by how they compare to others. In a competitive model, there is always another competition down the road, and position and stature are only as secure as the results of that next exam. Not only did this teacher's competitive model of reward and humiliation help create more tension than usual during exams, but also it helped to make each student competitors of one another, hoping for each other's failure rather than their success.

This is an extreme yet nonetheless true story and a good example of how our classrooms and schools nurture competition rather than cooperation. By doing so, they help to create an atmosphere diametrically opposed to what is considered beneficial for learning and ultimately success. In the Carnegie Foundation's study of important skills for the twenty-first century, this is one of the skills it identifies: "the ability to work with others to solve problems." Even when, as in the dodgeball or survival show models, it appears there are two teams working against each other, it all comes down to one person winning and the rest losing. In this model, one uses the illusion of cooperation for individual purposes.

This is not about pretending that we don't live in a competitive world. It is only to emphasize that your school or classroom will have a more difficult time of achieving the kind of harmony you're after when a school's testing and teaching emphasizes competition at the expense of cooperation. While being number one or one of the best might encourage those few whose particular intelligence and background matches what is being tested, the majority of students who either don't appreciate competition or who are not precocious in a particular subject are quickly resigned to being failures. Any excitement they have for learning often goes down the drain.

Often, too, resentment and anger fester among students whose level of measured achievement is below those of the smart kids, and this can provoke jealousy and bullying. It is difficult enough to create a violence-free, diversity-celebrating classroom. It is even more difficult when schools provide very few ways that kids with diverse strengths can demonstrate those skills, so kids feel left out, unappreciated, and demoralized.

Understanding that our national model for assessment is still test-based, one that pits one school, district, and child against another, and that everything from real estate prices to textbook and test company profits play into this, we can still make some small steps toward a curriculum that supports the social goals you are trying to create. Here are some ideas:

- Create opportunities for cooperative work, preferably ones that use many skills.
- In physical education, find games that require teamwork. The New Games curriculum did just that, turning gym class from dodgeball and to cooperative problem-solving.
- Theater and dance lend themselves to activities that require group effort and cooperation. Bread and Puppet Theater, perhaps the most famous and influential theater in the last fifty years in America, chose to base its work on puppets so large that no one person could be the star and that a successful show required the cooperation of all. Finding or writing pieces where ensemble work is emphasized and where students can work together to create sets, backdrops, and so on is a good way to encourage cooperation.
- In music, parts that require limited skills yet fulfill important roles can be created. For instance, incorporate everyday sounds into composed pieces.
- Find opportunities to study where great ideas came from. In science, teach the social context of breakthroughs: Who was in the lab? What were the ideas from which the breakthrough idea emerged? In art, teach about the circle of artists who contributed to those styles that suddenly dominated art production: Did Jackson Pollock come down from heaven to paint his drip painting, or did his work evolve through his visits to the art studios of others or to museums or through his evolving interest in Eastern philosophy?
- In history, we tend to memorialize the "great men" and occasionally women. Just check out the "men on horseback" war statues around the country if you don't believe me. Spend some time studying the efforts of groups of people who made history: unions, the American and other revolutions, and

ecologically oriented pressure groups. Study how many people are needed to make a political campaign a success.
- In your science curriculum, look at studies that reveal how cooperation has been an essential part of how nonhuman species have flourished (see my introduction for some titles).

In order to change school culture, its curriculum and pedagogy must change, as well. Without this alignment, you will have a much more difficult job. It is more difficult for students to guide their behavior from an understanding of how we're all in it together when the curriculum romanticizes the individual and the pedagogy supports competition and isolated learning. We need to provide students with the experiences and intellectual fodder to help them realize that cooperation is not only possible but also a practical reality, with roots in nonhuman and human behavior and intellectual credentials as powerful and deeper than those that support a competitive model.

Chapter Ten

The Mouse's Problem and Yours!

A farm is a pretty nice place for a mouse to live, and this particular farm and this particular mouse went together particularly well. Mouse had it really good, plenty of after-meal crumbs on the floor and plenty of friends. Every morning after he awoke, Mouse walked around the barnyard, saying hi to his friends.

"Good morning, Cow," Mouse said.

"Good morning, Mouse."

"Good morning, Pig."

"Good morning, Mouse," Pig would grunt.

"Good Morning, Chicken."

"To you, too, Mouse."

Good friends and good food. What more could a mouse ask for?

Mouse's only problem on this farm was, of course, cats! In fact, there was one particular cat whose very presence sent shivers down Mouse's spine and made his heart beat *very* quickly. Luckily for Mouse, there were plenty of holes in the walls where he could scurry for safety as Cat made his inevitable rush toward him. Each morning, after a nice breakfast of pancakes and eggs, Farmer Don and Farmer Heather put their dishes into the sink, washed the table down with a wet cloth, and went about their business, leaving, as usual, a few tasty scraps on the floor.

Hanging out inside one of his holes, Mouse, once he was confident that the farmers had left, went into the kitchen and feasted on the pancake crumbs, some even moist with maple syrup! He enjoyed eating so much that he almost didn't hear Cat dart through the swinging screen door straight toward him. Mouse dropped a nice, thick piece of pancake and ran, his heart beating *very* fast, into the hole and to safety. Mouse, whose heart continued to beat *very* fast, sat in the security of his mouse hole, until Cat, realizing that this was just not his day, left. When he did, Mouse's little heart finally slowed down.

Into the kitchen, however, walked Farmer Don and Farmer Heather, who were talking very excitedly and angrily, and their conversation made Mouse's heart beat *very* fast again.

"I just saw some mouse droppings near the walnuts!" said Farmer Don.

"Yes," answered Farmer Heather. "I do think we have mice. I just saw droppings near the flour!"

"We have to get that mouse," said Farmer Don.

"You're right," said Farmer Heather. "I'm going to set a trap now!"

Mouse began to twitch and shake as he saw Farmer Don leave the kitchen and watched Farmer Heather set the mouse trap with a nice big hunk of a juicy bleu cheese as bait.

"Bleu cheese?" thought Mouse. "I haven't had bleu cheese in years. I *love* bleu cheese! What am I going to do? Once Farmer Heather leaves, and after I finish digesting my breakfast, I will be hungry again and go right to that bleu cheese and then—thwak! That'll be it for me! I have no self-control when it comes to bleu cheese. None! I need some advice about what to do. Good thing I have some smart friends like Cow, Pig, and Chicken. They'll know what to do."

Mouse waited until Farmer Heather's back was turned and then scurried out the door. He came to his friend Cow, who was out in the field, chewing on her cud.

"Cow, may I speak with you a minute?" asked Mouse.

"Why sure, Mouse, but make it quick. As you can see, I'm very, very busy!"

"Look, Cow, I have a problem. You know how much I love bleu cheese? I've told you, right?"

Cow nodded her head yes.

"Well, Farmer Heather is at this very minute, *this very minute*, setting a trap for me *loaded* with bleu cheese, and I'm afraid that, because I have no willpower when it comes to bleu cheese, I'm going to go for that cheese and then—thwack! And then, you'll never see me again! Cow, what'll I do?"

Cow stood there, chewing her cud and brushing flies off her back with her tail, and finally said, "Mouse, sorry I can't help. It's just not my problem."

Mouse went over to see Chicken, who was peck, peck, pecking away at the ground.

"Chicken. Chicken, I'm sorry to bother you, but I have a problem. Listen, I just heard Farmer Don and Farmer Heather talking, and they noticed that I've been feasting off their walnuts and flour, and they were none too happy about it, and well, they've decided to set a trap for me filled with—bleu cheese. Yes, bleu cheese, and you know how much I like it, right? I have no self-control when it comes to bleu cheese. None! We've talked about it, right? So, as you can imagine, I'm afraid that I will go right for that cheese once I'm hungry or maybe even before and then—thwack! That trap will come down on me, and that will be the last of Mouse. What's your advice?"

Chicken kept on peck, peck, pecking and finally looked up for a second and said, "I sympathize with you Mouse, I really do, but as you can see, I'm quite busy, and you know, that's really not my problem."

Mouse went over to Pig, who seemed to be having the greatest time of his life, rolling, rolling, rolling in the mud. He was laughing so hard that his whole body shook like Jell-O.

"Oh, excuse me, Pig. I'm sorry to bother you. You seem to be having so much fun, but I have a problem. I just overheard Farmer Heather and Farmer Don talking, and it seems that they are going to set a trap for me and use my *favorite* cheese, bleu cheese, as bait! I just love bleu cheese. *Love* it! Can't get enough of it, and I know with my willpower, as low as it is, I'm going to go for it as soon as I see it laying there, and then that bar's going to come down and—thwack!" Mouse was shaking so hard imagining himself beneath the trap's metal bar that he couldn't get his words out. His little body shook, and his heart beat faster and faster, and the only thing that he could finally say was, "What can I do?"

Pig was so enjoying his roll in the mud that he couldn't stop, but he did manage four words, four words now familiar to Mouse: "It's not my problem."

Suddenly Mouse heard the sound of the mousetrap snapping shut. Who could that be? He hoped it wasn't that cute girl mouse he'd seen outside the other day. He scurried toward the kitchen and carefully looked in and was happy to see it wasn't the cute girl mouse caught in the trap. It was, instead, a snake, who must have slithered into it by mistake, and there was Farmer Heather lifting the trap's bar carefully to free it. But, the scared snake reared back her head and bit Farmer Heather, who dropped the snake and the trap and screamed. By the time Farmer Don ran into the kitchen, his wife was on the floor.

"A snake bit me!" she said.

Watching the snake slither out the door into the yard, Farmer Don realized that it had indeed been a poisonous snake that had just bitten his wife. He carried his wife into bed. With his wife deteriorating, he knew he had to give her something to eat, something to fill her body with nourishment, something that would help her fight off the poison from the snake's bite! He walked outside and called out, "Come here, Chicken."

Chicken, anticipating some more grain, obediently followed that voice, and in a mere second after she arrived, with a swift and strong hand, Farmer Don grabbed that chicken, placed her on a chunk of wood, and chopped her head off with a swift blow. He took the chicken's body inside, pulled out the feathers, cleaned it up, boiled some water, cut up some vegetables, and put the chicken inside the pot with the vegetables. About an hour later, after adding some salt, pepper, a little garlic powder, and some bay leaves, there it was: chicken soup.

Delicately and patiently, he fed the soup to his ailing wife, but after a number of bowls, Farmer Heather was not getting better. Realizing that she might need some more food, Farmer Don went into the barnyard, where Pig was still happily rolling in the mud.

"Come here, Pig!"

Farmer Don made some pork chops, ham, and pork roast and fed it patiently to his ailing wife. Even though Farmer Heather ate and ate, it was unfortunately to no avail. The hard-working and loving Farmer Heather succumbed to the poisons in her body and was soon just a memory. She passed away, and it was time to invite the entire village over for the funeral. The villagers needed to be fed at the funeral, and with all that had occupied Farmer Don these many days, he had not had time to shop. So, he went into the field, and he loudly called. Cow was turned into roast beef, steak, and pot roast that fed the villagers as they mourned the passing of Farmer Heather.

Mouse, a careful observer to all that had gone on from the time he heard the "Thwack!" of the trap to the sight of the last tear at the funeral, realized that he had learned something from it all: Whenever you say to someone in trouble that their problem is not yours, remember, even though it doesn't seem so at first, it just might just be!

QUESTIONS FOR STUDENTS

- Did the ending surprise you? If so, how else did you imagine this story would end?
- Have you ever watched or laughed when someone was bullied or teased and didn't do anything because you thought it wasn't your problem?
- Do you find it difficult to stand up for someone? If so, why? Were you ever worried that you would make things worse by getting involved? If so, what were you worried about?
- Have you ever come to the aid of someone? If so, what did you do and how did you feel afterward?
- Have you seen any movies or read any stories about people getting involved in other people's problems? Which ones, and how did they do it?

THOUGHTS FOR STUDENTS

This parable is about one of the hardest things to do in life: getting involved when someone else is suffering from teasing, bullying, harassment, and so on, while you worry about what will happen to you if you do. It often seems so much easier to walk away than to risk your own health or status by getting involved. I've certainly been there, done that. I remember a time when a kid in junior high was bullying another kid who was not nearly as strong. It took place in an alley behind school. I was walking with my friend Lenny, and he stopped and told the stronger kid to stop picking on the one who was weaker. The bully responded by asking Lenny if he wanted a punch as well. I could have said something, but I felt that it was not my fight, and I pushed Len to walk away. It haunts me to this day.

Getting involved when you feel an incident is not your concern, especially when there is a very real chance of violence, is a very difficult thing to do. Yet, there have been quite a few people who *have* overcome their fear and intervened. There were Germans, Polish, Dutch, and more who hid Jewish people during the Holocaust at potentially great cost to their families and to themselves. The same is true for some whites and free black people who helped fugitive slaves from the South travel to safety in the North and to Canada. There were those who went from the North to the South during the 1960s to help African Americans secure the right to vote. A few of these Freedom Riders died because of their involvement, while many who fought for equal rights and justice were hurt and even had their children killed.

In this parable, each animal approached by Mouse didn't want or didn't have the time to get involved. Why not? Well, they were all too busy and thought that Mouse's problem was not their own.

Is someone else's problem yours? That's a good question because, on the surface, in this particular story, it really didn't seem that Mouse's problem concerned Chicken, Pig, or Cow. But, it turned out it was their problem, wasn't it? For me, the story proved that ultimately one person's problem can easily become a problem for everyone.

Something seemingly as simple as keeping the air conditioner on when you leave the house has consequences for everyone else. The always-on air conditioner burns fossil fuels that contribute to global warming, which in turn damages crops, which in turn cuts the food supply somewhere in the world and at the least raises prices for you (to say nothing about the potential for melting the polar ice caps and flooding much of the coastal world).

Just as it is difficult to see the direct connection between the seemingly innocent act of leaving the air conditioner on in an empty room, someone teasing another would seem to have little effect on you. Teasing that is indulged, endured, or actively supported can spread like a wildfire in your classroom or school until no one feels safe. Everything and everybody becomes vulnerable in an environment where malicious teasing is OK'd by the silence of others, a silence that clearly says "It's not my problem."

One person's problem *is* another's problem. Just as the positive environment we spread comes back to us, the negative one we allow to fester becomes part of our world, as well. There are no neutral decisions. No choice is without consequences. That, of course, does not mean that you jump into a fight and pop any bully in the face. It means only that you think smartly about what to do next. Do you tell an adult? Do you and your friends refuse to be the bully's or the teaser's audience? The particular strategy is up to you. Make sure that your choice doesn't escalate the violence but instead helps to create a culture of caring where everyone understands that the world they create is the one they will inhabit.

THOUGHTS FOR TEACHERS

In some ways, this story tells it all. It is a story about how one person's problem is ultimately everyone else's. From this understanding, a strategy for an intrinsic character education curriculum based on deep individualism, mutual dependency, and the knowledge that we are indeed all in it together can be created.

Everyone is affected by the behavior and problems of others. Whether it's the sudden disappearance of your newspaperman's less-than-cheery morning hello because his house is underwater, a child coming into your classroom tired and in a disruptively bad mood because his parents had a late-night argument fueled by economic insecurity, or your friend's concern over what to do with her increasingly sick parent, it is clear that no one lives outside of a vastly integrated network of human beings, animals, and plants. Something happening in a distant part of the world ultimately affects everybody, and any individual's behavior affects the lives of others and, again, themselves.

This is indeed the lesson that drives the ultimate goal of this book: to teach experientially and academically that our lives are in continual dialogue with others, fully and irrevocably nested within a social and ecological context. Everyone truly depends on the health and well-being of everyone else for our individual health and well-being.

Here are some final suggestions for aligning your academic and social curriculum: Get rid of the silos! If you are teaching Dickens in English, read about the industrial revolution in social studies. If you are studying cubism, look at how nineteenth-century changes in the speed of new forms of transportation altered how the world was experienced. If you are studying Hurricane Katrina, look at the engineering choices made by the Army Corps of Engineers. If we are looking at how nonnative species affect our ecology, study how plants came into our country through international trade.

This kind of teaching is not without precedent and examples. In the November 14, 2016, edition of the *Big Think*, there is an article by Teodora Zareva, "The Latest School Reform in Finland Introduces a New Way to Look at Subjects," about recent changes in Finland's education. With its new National Curriculum Framework 2016 (NCF), Finland emphasizes the importance of a multidisciplinary approach to education and introduces the concept of phenomenon-based teaching, which will result in classes on broader topics, such as the European Union, climate change, and community.

By teaching in this way, you will help your students learn how to make connections and understand how cause and effect is not linear (one thing leading to the other) but more like a liquid matrix of mutually affecting interrelationships. This kind of teaching trains minds to notice, as William Blake said, "everything in a grain of sand." To look at the world as interconnected, mutually dependent, and continually evolving is to intellectually set the table for an understanding of how our behavior ultimately affects ourselves. With this holistic understanding of our relationship to each other and to our planet, it hopefully will be no longer possible to imagine that throwing a bottle out a car window or refusing to come to someone's aid will be without consequences to ourselves.

Only in a world where there is the mistaken belief that our actions have no consequences is everything permitted. Once it is recognized that our responsibility to others and our responsibility to ourselves are the same, choices based on momentary expediency, with no attention paid to consequences, will seem absurd and, truth be told, obscene. Once this understanding, that we all live in the same closed system, has soaked into the minds, hearts, and bodies of our students, our need to rely on extrinsic admonitions to create a culture of caring will be greatly decreased.

Martin Niemöller (1892–1984), a prominent Protestant pastor who was an outspoken enemy of Adolf Hitler and spent the last seven years of Nazi rule in concentration camps, uttered this famous quote apropos to the story in this chapter. It is a very simple way to understand how intertwined our fates are and that we are all dependent on each other for our health, happiness, and freedom—and how we are all in it together!

> First they came for the Socialists, and I did not speak out—
> Because I was not a Socialist.
> Then they came for the Trade Unionists, and I did not speak out—
> Because I was not a Trade Unionist.
> Then they came for the Jews, and I did not speak out—
> Because I was not a Jew.
> Then they came for me—and there was no one left to speak for me.

Conclusion

CONCLUSION FOR STUDENTS

Thank you for reading *Changing Curriculum through Stories: Character Education for Ages 10–12*. I hope that you liked it. Here are a few ideas to help you keep it together and to help everyone, including yourself, feel happier and more comfortable in school and out.

- Think for a second before you let anger or frustration dictate your behavior. Take a deep breath. Walk away. Make a joke. Hum a song. It doesn't matter which technique you use; just find a way to delay acting until your rational side takes control over your emotional response. The truth of your initial reaction melts like an ice sculpture on a sunny summer day when you have a little time to reflect.

  Don't be fooled by the power and false certainty of your initial reaction. Immediate reactions are like a little kid who won't shut up. "Me, me! Pay attention to me! Do what I tell you to do! Do what I tell you to do! Listen to me! I'm right!" Don't worry. Eventually this little kid gets tired of screaming, as long as you don't feed it by acting on its advice. In fact, if you feed it, it becomes hungrier! The most important thing you can do when you are angry, frustrated, or feeling hurt or disrespected is to consider the long-term effects of your action. Ask yourself this question: Will this really get me what I want?

- Decide that you will not bully or tease others to enhance your power or status, nor will you use others as punching bags to make you feel better when you are angry or down. Not only does no one deserve to be treated badly, not only would *you* not want to be used in that way, but also this type of behavior won't get you what you're after.

Bullying or teasing a weaker person does not enhance your reputation. You will appear weaker, less in control, and more insecure. The temporary rush you might get when you trip, push, or tease someone disappears very quickly.

Negative behavior or hating not only won't solve whatever emotional issues you think it might cure, but it also covers up what you are actually feeling and makes it more difficult to see what your real problem is and how you might successfully deal with it. Ask yourself what's really bothering you and why you feel it necessary to export your bad feelings to another person. What are these feelings of sadness, tensions, and insecurities that are stoking your anger? Where are they coming from, and what would be a healthier way for getting your real needs met?

- Remember, you are never invisible to yourself or to others. I know that sounds funny, but what I mean is that when you stand around and allow others to be bullied or teased, or when you join in on the fun, you are affecting the situation, and of course, you will ultimately be affected yourself. Standing by while others are teased or bullied, passing on a rumor, or purposely isolating someone is a strong and very visible statement of support for that action. It isn't easy to do otherwise. I know that from firsthand experience. Remember, courage is not about acting without fear but about recognizing the fear as you act to make another person's life better and you feel more powerful.
- Practice the joy of giving. Giving can be as simple as a short "How are you doing?" to someone who is down or as large as asking someone to participate in a game or to dance at a party when you sense they feel left out. Giving can mean helping out in a soup kitchen or teaching a skill to someone. It can mean standing up for someone who is being picked on or really listening and commenting on another kid's suggestions while you are his or her coworker in a group. It doesn't matter how you give to others; just remember that the more you give, the better and larger you feel.
- Appreciate the importance of your story. You are unique, interesting, complex, and a gift to those around you. We are all important, with lots to share and to contribute. Having the confidence to be who you really are is essential if your little part of the jigsaw puzzle of life is going to play its role in completing and also changing the grand puzzle. We all have our insecurities. Recognize them in yourself, and don't be afraid of them. Don't feel superior when you recognize insecurity in others. Remember, we all have our weak spots, and understanding that, try to create a culture in which we all feel OK about ourselves, even with our vulnerabilities and insecurities.
- Have a good time. Play music. Read. Play sports. Take walks in the city or in the woods. Go to the beach. See art. Get together with friends. Watch a

sunset. Go on a roller coaster. See the sunrise. Watch a storm come in. Plant a garden. Fix a car. Build a shelf. The more you take in the wonders of the world, the better you'll feel. The better you feel, the less important real or imagined slights, grudges, hurts, jealousies, envies, and resentments will seem. It is difficult to hold on to old anger when you are looking at a mountain lake at sunset. It is difficult to hold on to a grudge when you are effortlessly skating over a frozen pond.

• Remember, while it is difficult to change your own behavior, it is more difficult to change the behavior of others. Your responsibility is ultimately to yourself, making choices that fill you with energy, joy, surprise, and awe. Doing so will help you make decisions that will have long-term rather than short-term benefits, decisions that will help you create the kind of world you want to be part of. Remember, we're all in it together!

Good luck, and it was fun to spend some time with you.

CONCLUSION FOR TEACHERS

For every problem, there is opportunity—at least that is what wise folks say. Whether bullying is as big a problem as it is portrayed, it doesn't really matter. It does, nonetheless, affect many people. This gives all of you an opportunity to reframe your school-based discussions about character issues from admonition to those that can unite a school community around a shared interest in creating a culture of caring based on mutual benefit.

Our culture's current interest in school character issues comes at a time when wealth disparity in the United States is nearly exceeding all previous levels in history. It is occurring at a time when we seem unable to collectively decide that we must take action to stop or at least slow global warming. It is coming at a time of vast economic change, where a large part of our country's economy is based on Ponzi schemes and derivatives rather than manufacturing for the needs of its citizens. It comes at a time when more and more money is being stored in offshore hiding places that permit the wealthy to avoid contributing to the society into which they were born, where their talents were nurtured, and where they benefited from the work of previous generations. It comes at a time when political extremism threatens to tear the United States apart.

Attention to character education comes at a time when our entire country, not just our schools, is confronting who we are, the choices we are making, and whether our priorities and behavior should be altered. It is coming at a time when the results of acting from a shallow individualism—taking what you want, how you want, without regards to the long-term consequences for you, your family, and your world—is bringing our country and indeed our globe to the brink of destruction, slow or fast, depending on which kind of apocalypse you intellectually and emotionally favor. Consequently, as you approach these character issues in our schools, please understand that you are, with the proper depth and commitment, teaching nothing less than a rethinking of our culture's priorities and behavior, literally before it is too late.

None of us, anywhere on the earth, can any longer pretend that our individual actions have no consequences for the rest of us. Our work on character issues must make everyone a stakeholder in the effort to redirect behavior on both the individual and global levels. By teaching your students about character issues from the perspective of our interdependency within a closed system, we are teaching what it means to be responsible for our planet's future.

Here are some ideas for how you might extend the issues and suggestions discussed in this book:

- Use the stories and talking points in this book as jumping-off points for a school-wide conversation about behavioral issues.
- Allow your students to consider and suggest classroom and school policies for creating a culture where everyone feels supported and safe.
- Create a school-wide "Congress of Stakeholders" that includes all those who have a stake in the culture of the school (teachers, administration, lunch room and janitorial staff, parents) to address problems concerning bullying and teasing and their possible remediation.

    For instance, do students want to allow teasing? What kind of teasing is problematic, and how does one determine that some forms of teasing are friendly, while others are adversarial and violence-provoking? What should school policy be toward the type of teasing your community wants to eliminate? What should be the consequences of behavior that disregards these policies in general? How should consensus be reached? How should these policies be publicized? What are some ways to encourage compliance? How can these ideas and policies be continued and, if needed, altered year to year? How can you communicate with other schools in your area so that you can arrive at a consistent approach within your district and community?

There are many school-based mandates and lots of things that must be accomplished in a very limited amount of time. Making even minor changes to what and how you teach in order to emphasize how much we all have in common is a good start. Find opportunities to emphasize cooperation. Be aware of how you treat your students, staff, and peers; how respectfully you speak; how you defuse potential conflicts; how you share your laughter and attention; and how you solicit your students' thoughts and ideas.

Tell your own stories about how you bullied, were bullied, were teased, were left out, left others out, or passed rumors and how it affected and still has an effect on you.

Good luck with your work, and please know that no one minimizes the difficulty of what you do, underestimates your commitment, or fails to recognize the daunting task ahead for all of us.

A BONUS STORY FOR COMPLETING THIS BOOK . . . FOR STUDENTS AND TEACHERS!

The student asked her master, "What is the difference between heaven and hell?"

The master thought for a second and traveled with the student to a house where its inhabitants were sitting around a table filled with food. Surprisingly, people were starving. Their elbows were locked by a mysterious ailment and would not bend, and while they could grab the food in front of them, they were unable to bring it to their mouths.

Then the master brought the student to another house. It, too, was populated by people sitting at a table filled with food. These people were also afflicted with the mysterious ailment that left their elbows locked and unable to bend. But these people were all well-fed and happy. Like those in the other house, they, too, were able to grab the food in front of them, but unlike the others, they didn't try to feed themselves; instead, with their outstretched arms, they turned to their neighbors and fed each other.

May we all live inside such a banquet.

About the Author

Marc Levitt works at the intersection of the arts, education, and humanities. Mr. Levitt has been an author and storyteller for more than thirty years, and his work as a consultant and performer has taken him to more than sixty countries. His international work has been featured in the *New York Times*. Mr. Levitt has written *Putting Everyday Life on the Page: Inspiring Students to Write, Grades 2–7* (2009), a book about the teaching of writing. He created and directed for five years the innovative Charles N. Fortes Museum Project, based on site-specific education and funded by NEH/Disney Learning Partnership. For sixteen years, Mr. Levitt was the coproducer and host of the national award-winning radio show *Action Speaks! Underappreciated 20th-Century Dates That Changed America*. His two films, *Stories in Stone*, about the Narragansett stone wall–building tradition, and *Woven in Time: The Narragansett Salt Pond Preserve* have been broadcast on PBS stations throughout the United States. Both of Mr. Levitt's audio recordings, *Tales of an October Moon* and *Johnny Appleseed: Gentle Hero*, have garnered awards and positive reviews.

www.ingramcontent.com/pod-product-compliance
Lightning Source LLC
Chambersburg PA
CBHW020357270326
41926CB00007B/474